Walks Out of Shifnal

Paul Watts

© Paul Watts 2013

All rights reserved. No part of this publication may be reproduced, stored in a retrieval system, or transmitted in any form or by any means – electronic, photocopying, recording or otherwise – unless the written permission of the publishers has been obtained beforehand.

Disclaimer
At the point of printing it is believed that the contents of this book were correct. The publishers, however, cannot be held responsible for any errors or omissions. Nor can they be held responsible for any consequences by relying upon its contents.

The author has tried to be as accurate as possible with walk descriptions and each route has been walked by a team of independent walk-testers, but things do change so if the reader should find any anomalies or has any suggestions then contact is welcomed.

Further, the author has taken all reasonable steps to ensure that all walks are safe and achievable for anyone with an average level of fitness. However, all aspects of outdoor activity carry an element of risk and neither the author or the publishers can accept any responsibility for any injuries caused by following these walks.

ISBN 9 781489 530974

Front cover picture: King Charles's Wood from Kemberton Mill end.

Introduction

Here's a bold statement and a promise; this book will take you to places you've never been. Places you've never seen. Places you've never even heard of. But places you'll want to return to time and time again!

It's designed and created for all who are keen to discover the lovely countryside around the historic market town of Shifnal in Shropshire. Whether a family, a group or a solo walker – anyone interested in walking in the countryside will gain pleasure from this publication. And if anyone isn't - then let's hope they become inspired to do so, for there's just so much to see out there.

Just a glance at the Ordnance Survey Outdoor Leisure map 242 – Telford, Ironbridge & The Wrekin will reveal a network of footpaths, lanes and bridleways emanating out in all directions from Shifnal's busy centre. Walk east, west, north or south and the most splendid walks are there to enjoy. This book will help you explore them with its detailed walking instructions and maps, along with the wildlife to look out for and even a bit of the history that is Shifnal's fascinating heritage.

Since 2004 I've spent many happy hours walking the myriad of footpaths around this ancient market town, linking them to forge many delightful circular and linear walks from Shifnal's lively centre out through it's charming and fascinating countryside. And now, for the first time, I have written up my walks, drawn the maps and enlisted the help of a team of dedicated test-walkers to ensure that anyone who enjoys this lovely part of Shropshire's countryside can walk its tracks without fear of getting lost.

However, once out of Shifnal's busy centre, don't be surprised if you meet no-one. Many of the paths described are ancient right of ways, drovers routes and simple paths connecting hamlets and villages but their use over the centuries has much diminished and many have almost been forgotten. In days long since gone, Shifnal was an important staging post where weary travellers from the south on their way to Shrewsbury and as far as Holyhead would rest and stable their horses.

This has left a legacy, expanded in more recent years, bringing a network of superb footpaths and quiet lanes emanating out in all directions with woodland, small hills, quaint villages, secluded hamlets, remote pubs, tea rooms and delightful scenery ready to walk and enjoy. Let's walk these ancient tracks again and help to keep them open.

There are superb views on which to feast the eyes. For example, take the top of the very modest Lodge Hill (114 mtrs/374') where to the west can be seen Shropshire's most prominent hill – The Wrekin. To the south the Clee and Stretton hills. To the east lie the Malvern and the Clent hills.

The book features 23 walks, some circular, some linear appealing to walkers of all ages and abilities from solo walkers who might enjoy fairly long hikes in solitude, to rambling groups exploring this lovely part of Shropshire perhaps incorporating a pub lunch en route, to families who enjoy a short walk and a summer picnic. There really is something for everyone here.

Walks are all on easy terrain with very little climbing so all routes ignore what little there is of ascent in their timings. The only notable hills in Shifnal's immediate vicinity are Lodge and Nedge and no-one who is reasonably fit will feel too challenged by these.

The routes take in field paths, bridleways and quiet lanes with busier roads kept to an absolute minimum. The land around

Shifnal is a wonderful mix of arable, pasture and woodland. This means, of course, in wet weather some parts may be muddy. In the summer, some of the less used paths may be a little overgrown so carrying a stick may be useful to bash down a nettle or two. A stick is also useful to ward off Brown Bear and King Cobra who still linger around Shifnal, with packs of wild jackal still posing a problem! For those now concerned and perhaps put off from exploring these paths; I'm only joking – there are no longer packs of wild jackal.

The use of insect repellent during summer months is also strongly encouraged – horse flies being a particular bane of mine! (Although it has to be remembered that even the most painful and annoying of creatures is part of the rich diversity and ecology of our land – the glue that sticks the planet together).

Stout walking shoes or boots are also recommended at all times.

Contact with the author can be made through the website
walksoutofshifnal.com

How To Use This Guide

Choose between a linear or a circular walk and then select one that best fits your capabilities as far as mileage is concerned. Here's a challenge; aim to do them all, ticking each one off as you do them. Contact the author when completed.

The circular walks appear first in the book followed by the linear walks. Within each category the shortest walks appear first and finish with the longest. The shortest is just over 3 miles and the longest is 15.

As you follow the walks you will see that some descriptions are repeated across other walks as they share starts or finishes but each one is different and designed to bring out the best that Shifnal's surroundings have to offer. This makes each walk self-contained avoiding the necessity to flick through to follow sections of other walks as often happens in similar guides.

Maps & instructions
The routes described are designed to be easy to follow with the map as a confirmer and guide. The text is split into short paragraphs for ease of reading whilst walking.

At certain points where the route may not be obvious or is ambiguous a circled number on the map coincides with the same in the text. Routes cover lanes, footpaths and bridleways and are marked with a solid black line with various roads and footpaths leading off merely as confirmers.

Route ▬▬▬▬
Other road or lane
Other footpath or bridleway ·····················
Note ④

The text in italics carries interesting information about that section of the walk.

Each walk contains a map with detailed and thoroughly tested instructions but it is recommended that you take the relevant Ordnance Survey maps with you as a precaution. The map for all walks in this book is the 'OS Explorer 242 Telford, Ironbridge & The Wrekin'. Additionally, for the Badger Dingle and Bridgnorth walks, 'OS Explorer 218 Wyre Forest & Kidderminster' will also be required.

The maps in this book are to scale within themselves but not to scale with each other. This is because each map has been created to fit the page as large as possible.

Although it takes in most of the rights-of-way out of Shifnal this book isn't, and can never be, the definitive guide. Many more walks can be created using the OS maps and the reader is encouraged to devise others by linking walks described.

Quality of walks
Any book that features a series of walks will feature a small number that perhaps aren't quite as good as the others. For example there may be a short stretch of busy road, or the route may go through a housing area or trading estate. The less desirable route sections in this book have been kept to an absolute minimum but on occasions they are impossible to avoid and rather than leaving an otherwise superb walk out, 4 within this book are marked with this symbol…

✧

but please don't ignore them because other than a few less-than-inspiring minutes they are, nonetheless, superb walks.

Key
R = right.
L = left.
FP = footpath
BW = bridleway.
CP = car park.

Path Navigation
The vast majority of the footpaths and bridleways are well used and are therefore easy to navigate. However, there are some that are used very little and even others that appear to be completely unused but the instructions within each walk are detailed enough so no-one need worry unduly. In time, it is hoped, as more people acquire this book and start to use some of the little-walked routes, even the slightly obscure ones will become more open.

At the start of each walk along with the map is the walk number and the title which need no further explanation. There are 2 or 3 other snippets of information which need a word or two;

Distance
Although maps these days are produced in metric all walkers and most motorists prefer to use imperial when discussing routes so 'miles' rather than 'kilometres' are used in this publication. For similar reasons you will also see reference to yards and feet. I am fully aware that by doing this, due to EU regulations, I risk a heavy fine or imprisonment. So be it! As far as I'm aware, however, it's not illegal to read it!

Time to Allow
This is based on an average speed of 2 mph. This is purely a guide as some people will obviously walk faster and others will be much slower but after completing one of the walks,

assessment of all the others will be possible based on your own speed.

Refreshments
Pubs, cafes and tea rooms are mentioned and there are two things to check before the walk: In these times of much uncertainty for our village pubs particularly – is the pub still there? If so what are its opening times? Same applies for the tea rooms and cafés. Always check. Common sense really.

Transport
All walks start from the centre of Shifnal at the Millennium Clock in front of Katrina's Card Shop. At the time of publication free parking is available nearby;-
- Front of the shops (limited spaces and time)
- Behind the shops (access is down the side of the Spar/Post Office)
- Large car park behind the Co-op - accessed by driving along Aston Street (directly opposite Katrina's) a few yards and turning left. A little jitty brings you out at the side of the Co-op.

On linear walks there are suggestions for your return to Shifnal by using a 2nd car, bus, train or taxi.

Try **travelinemidlands.co.uk** for bus and train options to plan your return or to reach your start point at Shifnal centre.

Countryside Code – Revised 2004

- Be safe - plan ahead and follow any signs
- Leave gates and property as you find them
- Protect plants and animals, and take your litter home
- Keep dogs under close control
- Consider other people

To complement the book

For your convenience; download and print out individual walks - **walksoutofshifnal.com**

Acknowledgements

A huge THANK YOU to the team of walk-testers who diligently (and usually, happily!) tested all the walks in all weathers, made comments and in some cases re-walked them.

In order of number of walks tested

Jim Cox
David Williams
Keith Fowler
Jackie Fowler
Marilyn Hughes
Pam Greenwood
Julie Moore
Avril Simpson
Ron Murdoch
Aaron Cox
Les Hughes
Lindsay Ward
Richard Fennell
Sue Field

Without you this book wouldn't have been possible. I owe you one!

Also, a big thanks to Pam for her expertise in proof-reading. This means, of course, that if any typos and grammatical errors have slipped in – it's not my fault!

Circular Walks

		Miles	Page
1	The Lane Walk	3.2	13
2	Lodge Hill	3.3	17
3	Evelith Mill	3.7	21
4	Coppice Green	4.5	26
5	Kemberton Mill	5.4	30
6	Masons Arms at Kemberton	6.4	36
7	Grindleforge	7	42
8	Priorslee Lake ✧	7	49
9	Nedge Hill ✧	7.8	53
10	Ryton	8.4	59
11	Lizard Wood	8.9	65
12	The Bell at Tong	9.8	68
13	Seven Stars at Beckbury	11.1	72
14	Granville Nature Reserve ✧	11.7	80

Linear Walks

		Miles	Page
15	Weston Park	6.4	87
16	The Shrewsbury Arms at Albrighton	6.8	90
17	Granville Nature Reserve ✧	6.8	96
18	Ironbridge	8.2	97
19	Badger Dingle	9	104
20	White Ladies Priory & Boscobel House	9.2	109
21	The Fox at Chetwynd Aston	8.6	117
22	RAF Cosford Air Museum	10.2	122
23	Bridgnorth	15.2	130

21/7/18 1½ HRS VERY HOT DAY

Walk 1 – The Lane Walk
Distance: 3.2 miles
Time to allow: 1½ hrs without stops

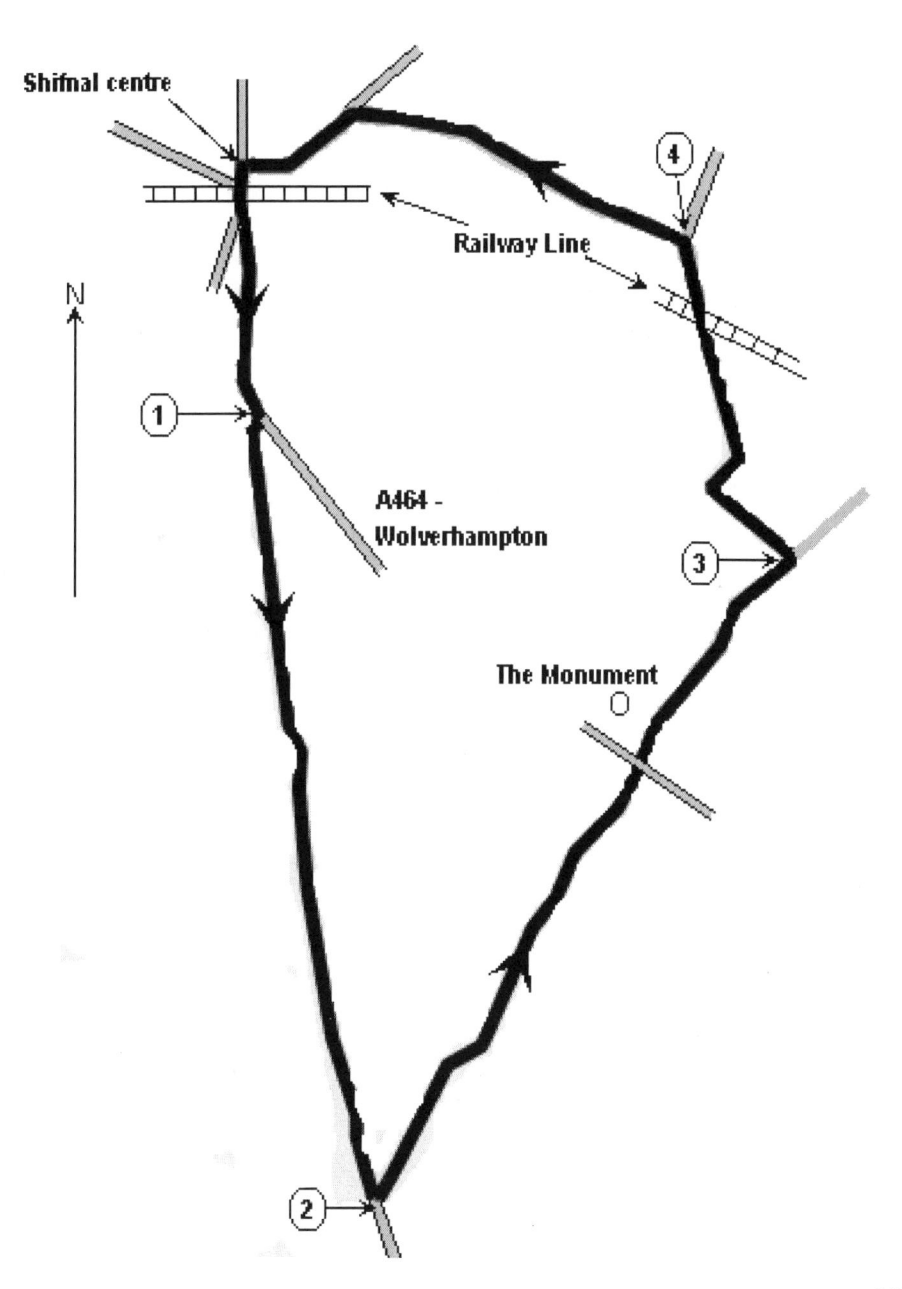

A short walk mainly on quiet lanes on the outskirts of Shifnal with one short stretch along a FP and maybe your first introduction to Shifnal's own hedge tunnel. More of this later, for there's much to see before you get there!

Start the walk from the centre of Shifnal at the Millennium Clock and head south under the railway bridge, passing the Odfellows pub and the Park House Hotel. As the road bends to the left turn R to walk up Park Lane ① (signed Ryton & Grindleforge), for about 20-30 minutes, past St Andrews School and alongside a superb row of mature trees of oak, sycamore, holly, horse chestnut and beech. In a while the houses disappear as the lane narrows and becomes much quieter.

NEXT ARRIVE AT HOUSE ON RIGHT ✓

Continue until you see a reddish sandstone wall on your right and shortly after you'll meet a lane on your L. Turn along the lane ② with fine views across a flat agricultural plain.

One sunny summer's day I spotted a grass snake here, sunning itself in the hedgerow. You will certainly see an abundance of wildflowers and hopefully a few butterflies too.

As you stroll along look ahead and to your right – do you see a flat topped silver-looking building? You can see it through gaps in the hedge. This is RAF Cosford's famous Cold War Museum.

As you continue round the twists and turns of this lovely quiet lane you will catch glimpses ahead of a large wooded area. This is Lizard Wood with Weston Park just to its right which is mainly in Staffordshire as the Shrops/Staffs county boundary runs right through it.

14

There are many fine old oak and ash trees lining the lane, but it's very much a mix of many species along here so if you have a tree identification book it's worth taking this along with you.

As you arrive at buildings and a farm be prepared to cross carefully the very busy and extremely fast A464. It's like the straight at Silverstone! However, once crossed, it isn't long before you're back into tranquillity as you walk ahead along a similar narrow lane.

If you look to your L you will see the remains of an old windmill (it may be obscured by the hedge in the summer but there's a gap further on) which over the years has become known as The Monument and is now linked in name to the Carp Fishery which we'll be passing shortly.

When you reach the brown leisure sign depicting a fish, turn L along this even narrower lane ③ to pass the entrance of the Carp Fishery and continue as it weaves R and then L leading then to a long straight where you'll eventually cross the Shrewsbury to Birmingham railway line at a hump-backed bridge. You might just be lucky enough to watch a train going under you.

From the bridge, looking L you can also see The Wrekin, Shropshire's most prominent although not the highest hill. If you look over R you will, once again, see the Cold War Museum framed between trees and a bridge, further along the railway line.

As you walk on you'll be aware that you're now entering part of Shifnal's industrial area with units on both sides of the lane. At a wide entrance on your L look out for a FP sign close by (it may be partly hidden by a hawthorn tree) and turn L along it to walk with a wooden fence on R ④.

INTO SEVERN TRENT & OTHERS

15

It's the only FP on the walk but it's a fine one – I think you'll see why in a moment. Continue along the path ignoring any other paths off as you head into a wonderful hedge tunnel. (No LONGER A TUNNEL AS NEW HOUSES ON THE LEFT)
But beware! There may be trolls. There are certainly dragons! In the autumn you'll also see some fine specimens of fungi, notably Miller, ceps and parasols. If you're really lucky you might even be able to pick hazel nuts but you'll have to be quick to beat the squirrels!

All too soon this magical diversion from the lane comes to an abrupt end as we enter a mix of residential and industrial properties. But stop a few seconds and turn around to look back and marvel at how this enchanting spot has naturally developed over the years with its canopy of foliage forging a hole right through, with of course, a little help from man. Maybe it's a disused railway line? I don't know but it makes for the culmination of this lovely lane walk.

CROSS OUT OF NEW HOUSES TO WIDER PATH OPPOSITE

As you continue past the gardens of a row of terraced houses on your R the path widens. Eventually turn R on to a concrete drive and on to Aston Street where you turn L and head back into Shifnal Centre and the return to the Millennium Clock. There is a Notice Board near the clock, by the way, which is certainly worth a read as it details some of the history and points of interest of Shifnal Town.

Walk 2. Lodge Hill Circular

Distance: 3.3 miles
Time to allow: 1¾ hrs without stops
Refreshments: Pubs and tea rooms in Shifnal

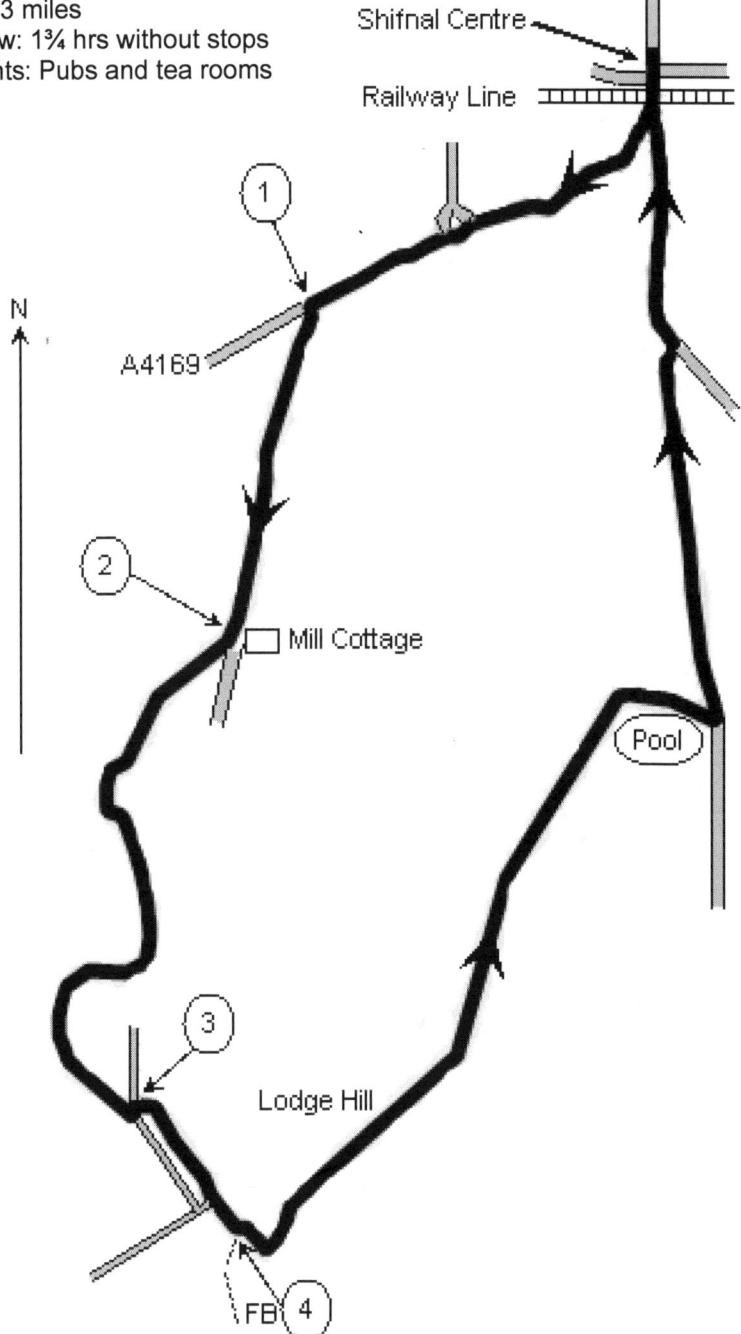

17

A lovely short walk through fields, lanes and woodland which can be enjoyed by all the family (although not recommended for buggies).

Start the walk from the centre of Shifnal at the Millennium Clock and head south under the railway bridge. Opposite Odfellows Pub turn R down Church Street and follow past Old Idsall House on the R – reputed to be the oldest dwelling in Shifnal - past the church to reach a traffic island. Cross over to go along one of the main routes out of Shifnal (A4169). Walk along this busy road for around 350 yards and turn L just past East house ①. This is a lovely quiet, unnamed drive leading to Shifnal Manor and Manor Barns.

Away from the noise and activity of the road and Shifnal you're immediately plummeted into tranquillity. This delightful lane leads eventually to a fork just past Mill Cottage ②.

This is the site of a watermill which would have been behind the cottage. As you walk on take the R fork (the L fork is a private lane leading to the 15 century Shifnal Manor which you'll see ahead to the left).

We head towards a courtyard of tastefully converted barns. Just before the entrance with stables on your L take the FP on R which skirts the properties and soon turns R downhill towards woods.

Just through the metal gate at the bottom the path splits into two. The original one is on the L and follows the line of the Severn Trent sewerage plant. A new one to the R has been formed, I suspect, by regular walkers which goes through the trees. They meet several yards on – choose whichever you wish!

In April/May this little wooded area is awash with bluebells and is a place loved by many birds and insects. At any time of the year look out for shieldbugs in the nettles, docks, brambles and ground ivy as you exit the copse.

A little further on take a moment to marvel at the reed bed through the fence. Like most modern sewers a reed bed is incorporated as part of the water cleansing process. The reeds bring huge amounts of oxygen through their stems into the roots which give life to the micro-organisms turning them into detritus-eating machines completing the purification process.

The wood changes to a hedge on your R. Looking ahead you'll see tree-topped Lodge Hill, a climb you'll be doing later. When the path ends at a lane, cross over heading slightly L downhill to reach a FP on the other side ③ which heads downhill through woodland once more.

Many years ago a paper mill stood in this area which relied on the force of the brook to drive a waterwheel, but little (If anything) now remains.

The path soon rises slightly to reach a junction with a farm track. Turn L down this wide, often muddy, track which soon peters out to a FP near the bridge over Wesley Brook.

④ Cross the bridge and follow signs to climb George's Steps (look out for the sign on a tree to your L) to a wooden seat at the top. The path ends at a stile just a few yards on, to a field with the hill before you.

Lodge Hill – the sting in the tail of this short walk – rises in front of you. Head straight up the hill on a faint path keeping close to the fence on L.

Despite the fact that Lodge Hill is a short climb there are great views back over to the Clee Hills to the south and Clent Hills to the east. On a clear day you can also see the Malvern Hills in Worcestershire south of east.

Just past the wooded hill-top look closely at the northern edge of the trees and you should be able to pick out the Ordnance Survey triangulation pillar which marks the height of this modest little hill-top at 114 mtrs (374 ft).

A little further on, look back and to the west of Lodge Hill's trees and you will see Shropshire's most prominent hill – The Wrekin.

The path continues to a stile at a gate and opens into a long straight farm track, with hedge on left and fence on right, soon changing to fence on L and hedge on R. Eventually it swings R at the bottom hedge (just over another farm-track crossing it) and after a small pool on your R, deposits you on to Park Lane. Turn L and after some minutes, on reaching the junction with a main road, turn L to walk past the Park House Hotel, back to the centre of Shifnal and the Millennium Clock.

Walk 3. Evelith Mill Circular
Distance: 3.7 miles
Time to allow: 2 hrs without stops
Refreshments: Pubs and tea rooms in Shifnal

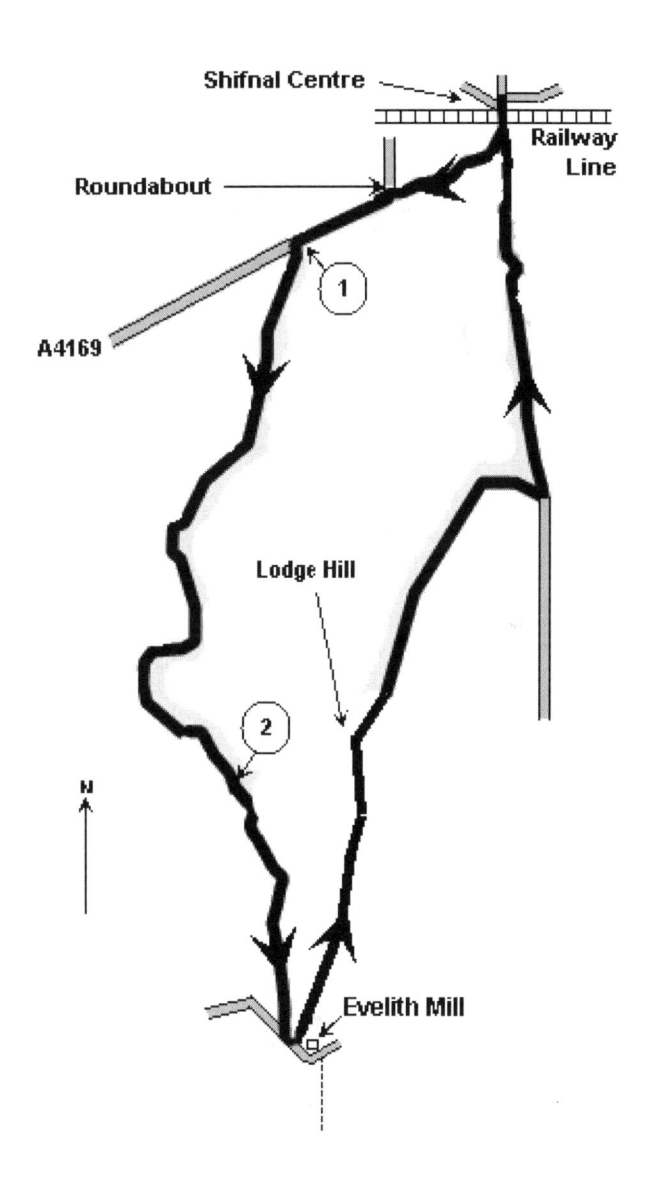

This little walk is a delight any time of the year but particularly during the spring and summer when it abounds with wildflowers and insects. It also passes sites of 2 water mills fed by the once powerful Wesley Brook which the walk encircles.

Start the walk from the centre of Shifnal at the Millennium Clock and head south under the railway bridge. Opposite Odfellows Pub turn R down Church Street and follow past Old Idsall House on the R – reputed to be the oldest dwelling in Shifnal, past the church to reach a traffic island. Cross over to go along one of the main routes out of Shifnal (A4169). Walk along this busy road for around 350 yards and turn L just past East house ①. This is a lovely quiet, unnamed drive leading to Shifnal Manor and Manor Barns.

Away from the noise and activity of the road and Shifnal you're immediately plummeted into tranquillity. This delightful lane leads eventually to a fork just past Mill Cottage and the site of our first watermill which would have been behind the cottage.

As you walk on take the R fork (the L fork is a private lane leading to the 15th century Shifnal Manor which you'll see ahead to the left). We head towards a courtyard of tastefully converted barns. Just before the entrance with stables on your L take the FP on R which skirts the properties and soon turns R downhill towards woods.

Just through the metal gate at the bottom the path splits into two. The original one is on the L and follows the line of the Severn Trent sewerage plant. A new one to the R has been formed, I suspect, by regular walkers which goes through the trees. They meet several yards on – choose whichever you wish!

In April/May this little wooded area is awash with bluebells and is a place loved by many birds and insects. Look out for shieldbugs in the nettles, docks, brambles and ground ivy as you exit the copse. At the right time of year you might also hear the drumming of a woodpecker and the call of the cuckoo.

A little further on take a moment to marvel at the reed bed through the fence. Like most modern sewers a reed bed is incorporated as part of the water cleansing process. The reeds bring huge amounts of oxygen through their stems into the roots which give life to the micro-organisms turning them into detritus-eating machines thereby making the final stage of purification complete.

The wood changes to a hedge on your R. Looking ahead you'll see tree-topped Lodge Hill, a climb you'll be doing later. When the path ends at a lane, ② cross over heading slightly L downhill to reach a FP on the other side which heads downhill through woodland once more.

Many years ago a paper mill stood in this area which relied on the force of the brook to drive a waterwheel, but little (If anything) now remains.

The path soon rises slightly to reach a junction with a farm track. Turn L down this wide, often muddy, track which soon peters out to a FP near the bridge over Wesley Brook. Do not go over the bridge but continue straight ahead.

This path alternately but gently rises and dips as it follows the brook on your L, until eventually it reaches the road at Evelith Mill passing a small rushing weir on the way. In the summer this is difficult to see through the foliage but you should be able to at least hear it.

When you reach the road turn L for a few yards and then L again through a gate which leads to a cottage *where you'll see the imposing Evelith Mill (built 1847) on your right with the remains of buildings which used to house the flour mill and water wheel again powered by Wesley Brook which must have been a great deal deeper, wider and faster than it is today.*

The path swings to the R around buildings and then L to a stile. Follow the obvious path through woodland as it rises and eventually, just through conifer trees, arrives at a paddock.

Climb this stile and then the other stile a few yards in front of you to alight onto a lane. Turn L here past a bungalow on your L towards the farm. When you reach farm buildings before the house turn slightly R to walk with the back of the farmhouse to your L and farm buildings to your right and you will see a stile in the line of oak trees ahead.

Lodge Hill – the sting in the tail of this short walk – rises in front of you. Climb the hill on a faint path heading towards the fenced and tree-covered top but turn right before you reach it along the obvious track.

Despite the fact that Lodge Hill is a short climb there are great views back over to the Clee Hills to the south and Clent Hills to the east. On a clear day you can also see the Malvern Hills in Worcestershire south of east.

Just past the wooded hill-top look closely at the northern edge of the trees and you should be able to pick out the Ordnance Survey triangulation pillar which marks the height of this modest little hill-top at 114 mtrs (374 ft). A little further on, look back and to the west of Lodge Hill's trees and you will see Shropshire's most prominent hill – The Wrekin.

The path continues to a stile at a gate and opens into a long straight farm track, with hedge on left and fence on right, soon changing to fence on L and hedge on R. Eventually it swings R at the bottom hedge (just over another farm-track crossing it) and after a small pool on your R, deposits you on to Park Lane. Turn L and after some minutes on reaching the junction with a main road, turn L to walk past the Park House Hotel, back to the centre of Shifnal and the Millennium Clock.

Walk 4. Coppice Green Circular
Distance: 4.5 miles
Time to allow: 2¼ hrs without stops
Refreshments: Pubs and tea rooms in Shifnal

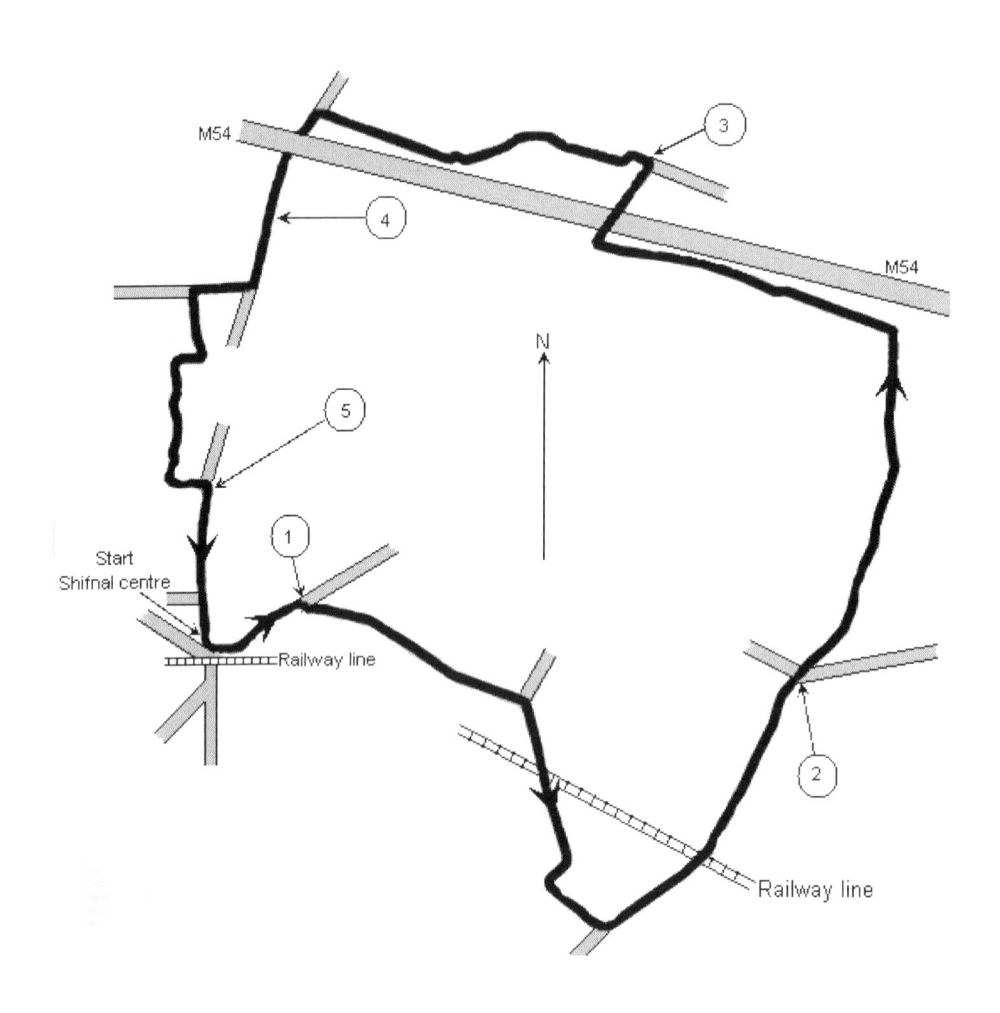

26

A short walk along footpaths, bridleways and country lanes, ending with an exploration of Wesley Brook as it flows through Shifnal.

Start the walk from the centre of Shifnal at the Millennium Clock. With your back to Katrina's Card Shop, cross the road and head along Aston Street with railway tunnels to your R and The Railway Inn and further on The Village Hall to your L.

When you reach Anvil Lodge ① turn R at the FP sign and then L to walk at the back of the Anvil Inn and houses. This wide drive soon reduces to a FP as you enter a charming hedge tunnel. Walk the length of this ignoring turns off until you reach a lane.

Cross in front of entrance to a large commercial building and turn R to take the lane slightly uphill to the bridge over the Birmingham-Shrewsbury railway line. Follow this narrow peaceful lane for a few minutes passing The Monument Carp Fishery on the R until you reach a junction with another lane. Turn L here and walk along this slightly wider lane, crossing the railway line again, to reach a main road. Cross carefully to the bridleway opposite. ②

This is a wide partly-surfaced track that is very pleasant to walk especially in spring and summer with wild flowers and insects in abundance. Soon, however, as Lizard Wood appears in front, the sound of the M54 affronts our ears.

The drive terminates on reaching the motorway and the path now turns sharp L to walk with hedge and motorway on R. Walk the boundary length of this very large field hugging the motorway.

The small wooded area up to your L is Aston Coppice and you will soon see Shropshire's most prominent hill - The Wrekin - in the distance.

Eventually, on reaching a hedge in front, the path turns L to a gate. Go through onto the road and turn R to cross over the motorway.

In a few yards a FP sign is seen just as the road bends R. This small area is known as Coppice Green ③. Here turn L and cross a stile to walk with a row of trees to your L to reach another stile. Cross in front of gates to a house and follow garden hedge on R and pool on L. Do not go through the small gate head but turn L round the edge of the pool to climb another stile. Turn R keeping the hedge on your R.

After a few minutes cross a stile over a footbridge and turn L keeping in the same direction with hedge now on your L.

Eventually reach another stile and a road. Turn L under the motorway bridge and take the surfaced path uphill L to walk in front of houses. This is Admirals Close ④.

On reaching the junction with Drayton Road turn R to cross over a main road, turning R to walk along Haughton Road. After a few yards turn L along Worfe Road. At the end of this short cul-de-sac take the FP between fences and when the R fence ends, turn R slightly downhill to a footbridge over Wesley Brook and a playing field.

Over the footbridge turn L to follow the brook on your L to a road. Cross straightover to FP, still following brook on L and houses both sides. Soon the path swings L to cross Wesley Brook over another footbridge.

Wesley Brook starts its journey at The Flash before flowing into Priorslee Lake and then right through the centre of Shifnal. It soon joins the River Worfe at Ryton which in turn flows into the River Severn near Bridgnorth, and eventually the Bristol Channel where it disgorges into the Atlantic Sea.

Over the footbridge follow the FP to reach a road ⑤. If in need of refreshment at this point the two closest hostelries are The Wheatsheaf to the R and The White Hart to your L. Otherwise turn R and follow the road back to the centre of Shifnal.

Walk 5. Kemberton Mill Circular
Distance: 5.4 miles
Time to allow: 2¾ hrs without stops
Refreshments: Pubs and tea rooms in Shifnal

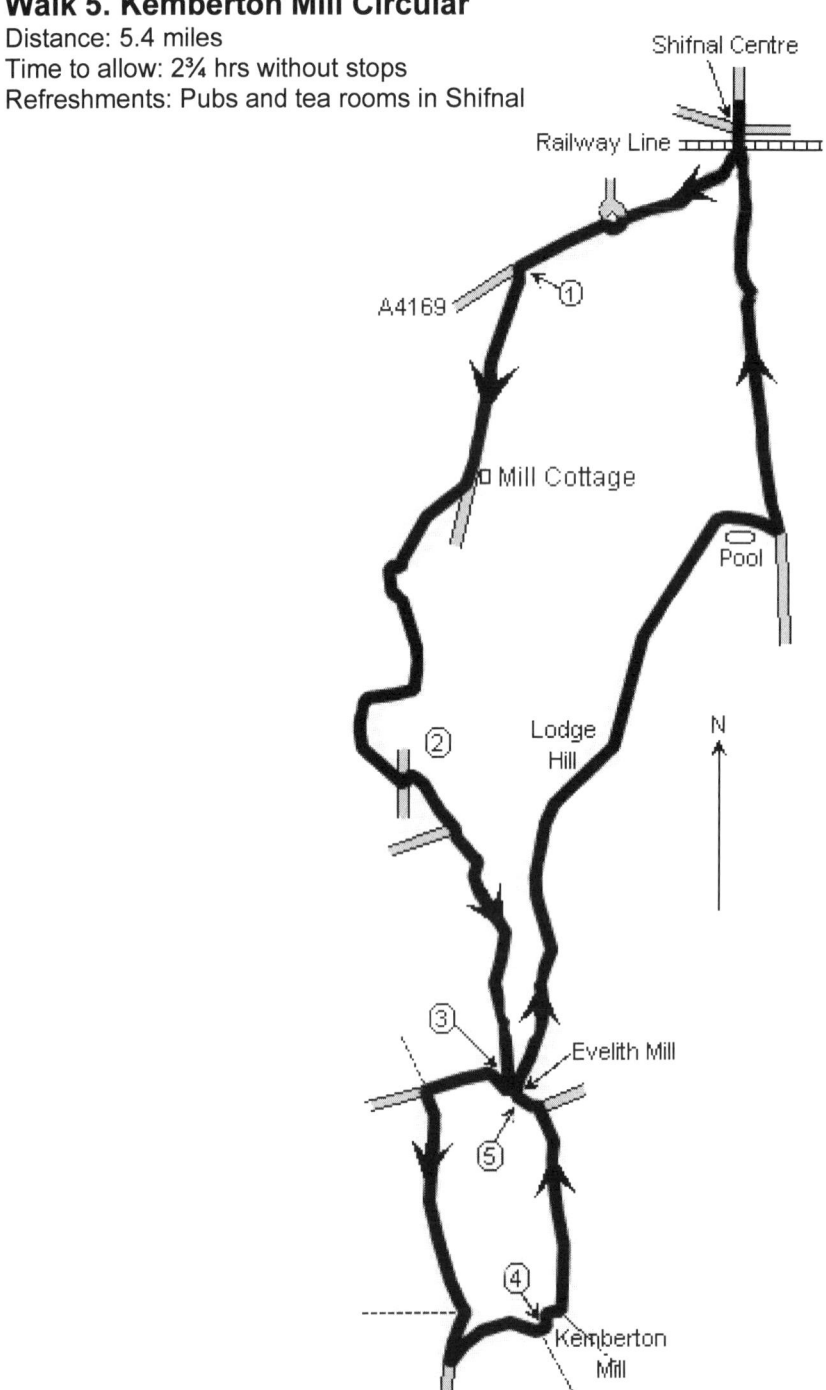

30

This walk is an extension of the Evelith Mill Circular which is in itself an extension of the Lodge Hill Circular and is more an elongated oval than a circular. This means you can tailor it entirely to your own needs as there are links across to the other side of the oval at strategic points but let's do the Kemberton Mill Circular in its entirety. It's a splendid walk for all seasons and one of my regular jaunts.

It also passes sites of 4 water mills fed by the once powerful Wesley Brook which the walk encircles.

Start the walk from the centre of Shifnal at the Millennium Clock and head south under the railway bridge. Opposite Odfellows Pub turn R down Church Street and follow past Old Idsall House on the R – reputed to be the oldest dwelling in Shifnal, past the church to reach a traffic island. Cross over to go along one of the main routes out of Shifnal (A4169). Walk along this busy road for around 350 yards and turn L just past East house ①. This is a lovely quiet, unnamed drive leading to Shifnal Manor and Manor Barns.

Away from the noise and activity of the road and Shifnal you're immediately plummeted into tranquillity. This delightful lane leads eventually to a fork just past Mill Cottage and the site of our first watermill which would have been behind the cottage.

As you walk on take the R fork (the L fork is a private lane leading to the 15th century Shifnal Manor which you'll see ahead to the left). We head towards a courtyard of tastefully converted barns. Just before the entrance with stables on your L take the FP on R which skirts the properties and soon turns R downhill towards woods.

Just through the metal gate at the bottom the path splits into two. The original one is on the L and follows the line of the Severn Trent sewerage plant. A new one to the R has been formed, I suspect, by regular walkers which goes through the trees. They meet several yards on – choose whichever you wish!

In April/May this little wooded area is awash with bluebells and is a place loved by many birds and insects. Look out for shieldbugs in the nettles, docks, brambles and ground ivy as you exit the copse.

A little further on take a moment to marvel at the reed bed through the fence. Like most modern sewers a reed bed is incorporated as part of the water cleansing process. The reeds bring huge amounts of oxygen through their stems into the roots which give life to the micro-organisms turning them into detritus-eating machines thereby making the final stage of purification complete.

The wood changes to a hedge on your R. Looking ahead you'll see tree-topped Lodge Hill, a climb you'll be doing later. When the path ends at a lane, cross over heading slightly L downhill to reach a FP on the other side ② which heads downhill through woodland once more.

Many years ago a paper mill stood in this area which relied on the force of the brook to drive a waterwheel, but little (If anything) now remains.

The path soon rises slightly to reach a junction with a farm track. Turn L down this wide, often muddy, track which soon peters out to a FP near the bridge over Wesley Brook.

Beware – for an old troll lives under the bridge! He's usually asleep so go quietly as you pass him by and all will be well. Shhhhh.

Do not go over the bridge but continue straight ahead. (Should the path be flooded which sometimes happens after heavy rain retrace steps, turn L on reaching the lane and then L to follow a Permissive Path above the dingle and rejoin the main path shortly).

This path alternately but gently rises and dips as it follows the brook on your L until eventually reaching the road at Evelith Mill ③ passing a small rushing weir on the way. In the summer this is difficult to see through the foliage but you should be able to at least hear it.

When you reach the road turn R to walk up the lane which soon levels out and reaches a FP with a rather awkward stile on the L. Climb down to walk with bank and trees on your L.

Keep a look-out around here for Brown Hare.

At the end of this long field you'll reach a stile by a well-positioned bench which catches the afternoon sun.

Cross the stile, follow the track to the R then turn L on reaching the lane. Follow this to the wonderfully isolated hamlet of Kemberton Mill which consists of just 2 houses. Just past Kemberton Mill Cottage take the FP on the L ④, signed Evelith Mill, which crosses in front of tumble-down buildings, one of which was the original mill and our 4th water mill on the walk.

Cross two bridges over the small weir and brook, then take the left-hand path to enter King Charles's Wood *so-called as it is recognised as part of King Charles II's route that he took after his defeat against Cromwell at the Battle of Worcester and forms part of the 615 mile long-distance path - The Monarch's Way.*

33

As you walk through this fine wood with Wesley Brook on your left you can imagine the somewhat panicked King and a few of his followers cantering through these trees in an attempt to greaten the distance between them and the determined men of Cromwell's army.

After some time the path ends at a lane where you'll see Evelith Mill ahead. Turn L to walk along the lane for a few yards. You are now close to the path you came in on but we're not taking that one! Two paths run either side of Wesley Brook and we're now going to be walking along the opposite side to the one we came in on. So turn R through a gate before the bridge ⑤ which is the drive leading to a cottage.

On the right you'll see the remains of buildings which used to house the mill and water wheel again powered by Wesley Brook which must have been a great deal deeper, wider and faster than it is today.

The path swings to the R around buildings and then L to a stile in a few yards.

Follow the obvious path through woodland as it rises and eventually, just through conifer trees, arrives at a paddock. Climb this stile and then the other stile a few yards in front of you to alight onto a lane. Turn L here past a bungalow towards the farm. When you reach farm buildings before the house turn slightly R to walk with the back of the farmhouse to your L and farm buildings to your R and you will see a stile in the line of oak trees ahead.

Lodge Hill – the sting in the tail of this short walk – rises in front of you. Climb the hill to the fence then turn R to follow the fence on your L still climbing.

Despite the fact that Lodge Hill is a short climb there are great views back over to the Clee Hills to the south and Clent Hills to the east. On a clear day you can also see the Malvern Hills in Worcestershire south of east.

Just past the wooded hill-top look closely at the northern edge of the trees and you should be able to pick out the Ordnance Survey triangulation pillar which marks the height of this modest little hill-top at 114 mtrs (374 ft). A little further on, look back and to the west of Lodge Hill's trees and you will see Shropshire's most prominent hill – The Wrekin.

The path continues to a stile at a gate and opens into a long straight farm track, with hedge on left and fence on right, soon changing to fence on L and hedge on R. Eventually it swings R at the bottom hedge and after a small pool on your R, deposits you on to Park Lane. Turn L and after some minutes on reaching the junction with a main road, turn L to walk past the Park House Hotel, back to the centre of Shifnal and the Millennium Clock.

Walk 6. Masons Arms at Kemberton - Circular

Distance: 6.4 miles
Time to allow: 3¼ hrs without stops
Refreshments: Masons Arms pub, Kemberton

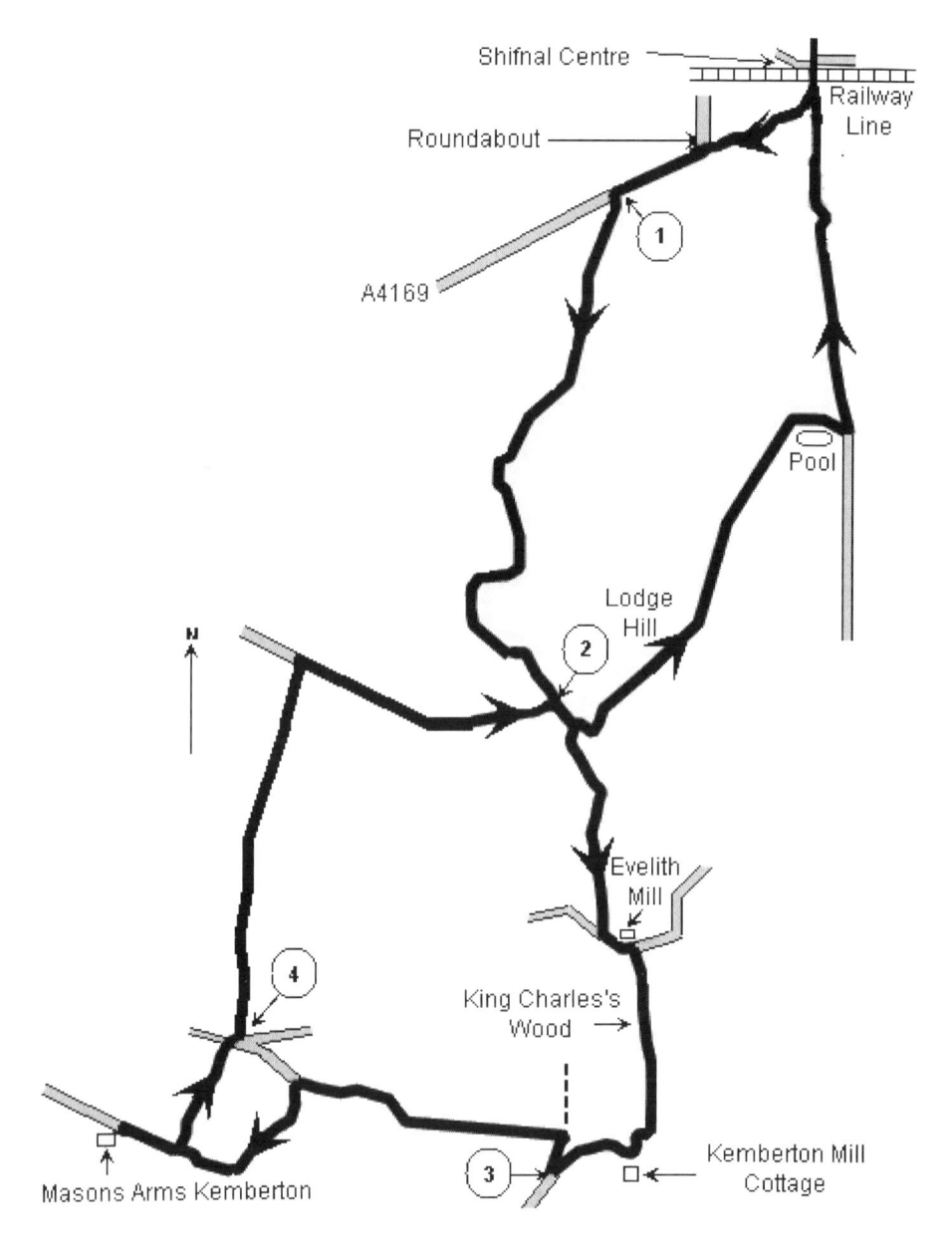

36

A lovely walk to a welcoming pub in the quaint old village of Kemberton. The Masons Arms is a 17th century pub with stunning views over the Shropshire countryside. On a warm day the garden is a delight. On a cold day the warmth inside is welcoming and homely and this circular walk takes in some of the best footpaths, bridleways and country lanes the area around Shifnal has to offer.

Start the walk from the centre of Shifnal at the Millennium Clock and head south under the railway bridge. Opposite Odfellows Pub turn R down Church Street and follow past Old Idsall House on the R – reputed to be the oldest dwelling in Shifnal, past the church to reach a traffic island. Cross over to go along one of the main routes out of Shifnal (A4169). Walk along this busy road for around 350 yards and turn L just past East house ①.

This is a lovely quiet, unnamed drive leading to Shifnal Manor and Manor Barns. Away from the noise and activity of the road and Shifnal you're immediately plummeted into tranquillity. This delightful lane leads eventually to a fork just past Mill Cottage and the site of a watermill which would have been behind the cottage.

As you walk on take the R fork (the L fork is a private lane leading to the 15th century Shifnal Manor which you'll see ahead to the left). We head towards a courtyard of tastefully converted barns. Just before the entrance with stables on your L take the FP on R which skirts the properties and soon turns R downhill towards woods.

Just through the metal gate at the bottom the path splits into two. The original one is on the L and follows the line of the Severn Trent sewerage plant. A new one to the R has been formed, I suspect, by regular walkers which goes through the trees. They meet several yards on – choose whichever you wish!

In April/May this little wooded area is awash with bluebells and is a place loved by many birds and insects. Look out for shieldbugs in the nettles, docks, brambles and ground ivy as you exit the copse.

A little further on take a moment to marvel at the reed bed through the fence. Like most modern sewers a reed bed is incorporated as part of the water cleansing process. The reeds bring huge amounts of oxygen through their stems into the roots which give life to the micro-organisms turning them into detritus-eating machines thereby making the final stage of purification complete.

Looking ahead you'll see the tree-topped Lodge Hill, a climb you'll be doing later. When the path ends at a lane, ② cross over heading slightly L downhill to reach a FP on the R which heads downhill through woodland once more.

Many years ago a paper mill stood in this area which relied on the force of the brook to drive a waterwheel, but little (If anything) now remains.

The path soon rises slightly to reach a junction with a farm track. Turn L down this wide, often muddy, track which soon peters out to a FP near the bridge over Wesley Brook. Do not go over the bridge but continue straight ahead.

This path gently rises and dips as it follows the brook on your L until eventually reaching the road at Evelith Mill passing a small rushing weir on the way. In the summer this is difficult to see through the foliage but you should be able to at least hear it.

On reaching the road turn L for a few yards passing the splendid white-pillared Evelith Mill (built 1847) on your L, once a flour mill complete with water wheel. In a few yards take the bridleway on the R through woodland.

This is King Charles's Wood so named as part of the route taken by King Charles II after he fled north, then east and finally way down south to Brighton and over to France following his defeat in the Battle of Worcester at Powick Bridge. This forms a tiny part of the 615 mile National Trail – The Monarch's Way.

Depending upon the time of year you may see squirrels and pheasants and hear the call of the Buzzard overhead. On a hot summer's day you enter this superb woodland to a refreshingly cool atmosphere dappled by sunlight as the rays streak through the foliage.

At the end of the wood turn R at a path junction, over a bridge and weir passing tumble-down buildings on the R to a lane at the delightful hamlet of Kemberton Mill and the site of yet another flour mill.

Turn R here to walk along the lane. After about 5 minutes take the FP on your R ③ which goes off at an acute angle to follow a hedge on your L. At the end is a stile, climb over to walk with a bench and fence on your R.

In a few yards at a marker on the blind side of a nearby tree take the FP on the L heading uphill across a large field towards a small electricity pylon. The field then levels and ends a short way past another tree. The actual FP continues straight ahead across the next field but this is rarely used as it is usually either ploughed or in crop, so the alternative (and much better option) is to turn R here along a track and then L when you reach the hedge. Follow the field edge alongside the hedge until reaching an opening onto a short track which is a Permissive Path ending at a lane.

Turn L here and walk along the lane for a few yards and then turn right on a FP at the side of Mid-Way House. Walk through the next field, ignoring a FP on R and continue along a grassy track and just as you reach a lone house take the FP on R and follow it L around the field perimeter, up the rise and eventually reaching a small gate at the top and then a large one leading to the road in the lovely village of Kemberton.

Cross straightover and walk up the lane ahead where The Wrekin will come into view in the distance. At the top of the hill you'll arrive at the Masons Arms for a well-earned pint or a glass of wine, or even a pint of wine! Don't overindulge though – there's still a walk and navigation to concentrate on for the journey back.

On leaving the Masons Arms retrace your steps down the road with church on L to the junction. Turn L and walk along the main road through Kemberton.

⑥ Just past the turning for High Farm, as the road bends right, turn L on to a FP.

The path runs the gauntlet between hedges to reach a gate and then our first stile of the walk. Climb a 2nd stile to walk straight across a field to a waymarked gap in the hedge which drops through trees. When, after a few yards, you reach a field turn R to walk with trees and then hedge on your R. After 2 fields you will reach a lane where you'll turn R to walk along it as Lodge Hill rises before you.

As the lane drops downhill it turns into a farm track. Turn R at the fork and walk down this wide, often muddy track, which soon peters out to a FP near the bridge over Wesley Brook.

Cross the footbridge over the brook and follow the path into woodland. Climb George's Steps (see if you can spot the sign on a tree to your L) and upon reaching the top you may want to dally a while on the seat set in the most perfect position after the short toil.

You now need to summon up enough energy to tackle the final 'up' of the day; Lodge Hill - the sting in the tail.

As you exit the wood at a stile, just head straight up the hill on a faint path keeping close to the fence on L.

Despite the fact that Lodge Hill is a short climb there are great views back over to the Clee Hills to the south and Clent Hills to the east. On a clear day, looking south of east, you can also see the Malvern Hills in Worcestershire.

Just past the wooded hill-top look closely at the northern edge of the trees and you should be able to pick out the Ordnance Survey triangulation pillar which marks the height of this modest little hill-top at 114 mtrs (374 ft).

A little further on, look back and to the west of Lodge Hill's trees and you will see Shropshire's most prominent hill – The Wrekin.

The path continues to a stile at a gate and opens into a long straight farm track, with hedge on left and fence on right, soon changing to fence on L and hedge on R. Eventually it swings R at the bottom hedge (just over another farm-track crossing it) and after a small pool on your R, deposits you on to Park Lane. Turn L and after some minutes on reaching the junction with a main road, turn L to walk past the Park House Hotel, back to the centre of Shifnal and the Millennium Clock.

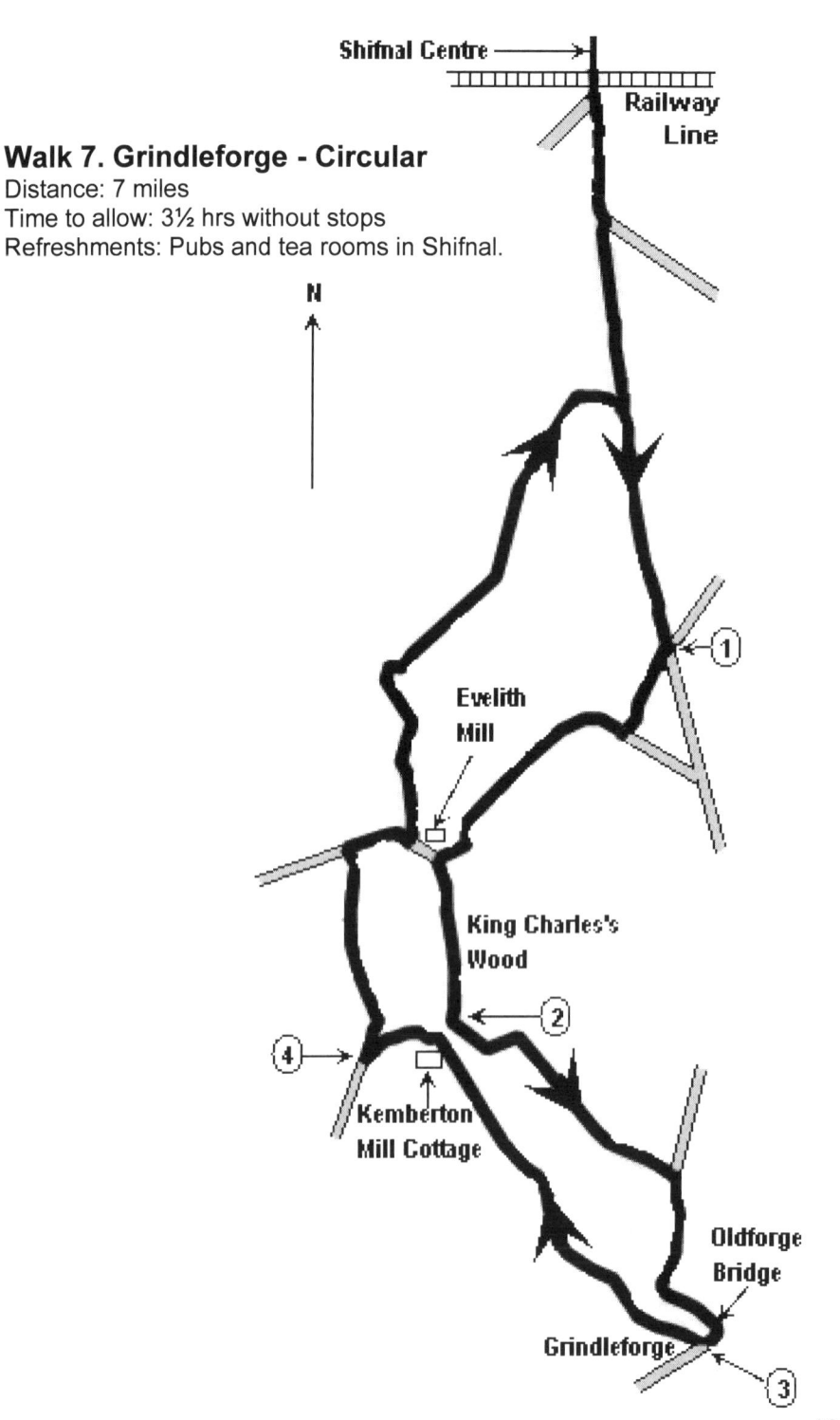

Walk 7. Grindleforge - Circular
Distance: 7 miles
Time to allow: 3½ hrs without stops
Refreshments: Pubs and tea rooms in Shifnal.

42

What a delightful walk this is! One of my regular walks from home and definitely one of my favourites. The countryside south of Shifnal is so varied with much to see and enjoy. This route takes in two ancient woodlands, the remains of two water mills and passes what was once the thriving Hinkesman's Hinnington Spring Brewery.

Start the walk from the centre of Shifnal at the Millennium Clock and head south under the railway bridge, passing the Odfellows pub and the Park House Hotel. As the road bends L turn R up Park Lane (signed Ryton & Grindleforge), past St Andrews School and walk alongside a superb row of mature trees of oak, sycamore, holly, horse chestnut and beech. Soon the houses disappear as the lane narrows and becomes much quieter.

Continue until you see a reddish sandstone wall on your right and shortly after you'll meet a lane coming in on your left. Look to the right to locate a FP sign. ①

Climb the stile and head diagonally across to the end of the tree-line ahead which actually forms the edge of a small copse. (Depending on the crop in this field it may be easier to take the path R that skirts the field). As you reach the corner and the end of the copse continue down, but slightly to the right, aiming for a telegraph pole and house.

Climb the stile to join Evelith Lane where you turn R. As you walk along look out for a wide gap in the hedgerow to your right and you'll see the tree-topped Lodge Hill – we'll be going over that later! Soon you will reach cottages and a double bend where the lane heads downhill. When you see Evelith Mill – the splendid white-pillared house on your right – take the bridleway on the left through woodland.

This is King Charles's Wood so named as part of the route taken by the king after he fled north, then east and finally way down south to Brighton and over to France after his defeat at the Battle of Worcester at Powick Bridge.

Depending upon the time of year you may see squirrels and pheasants, along with the call of the Buzzard overhead. On a hot summer's day you enter this superb woodland to a refreshingly cool atmosphere dappled by sunlight as the rays streak through the foliage.

At a path junction turn left ② slightly uphill towards a waymarked gate. Continue upwards keeping the wood on your L and gorse bushes on your R.

On sunny May to September days you may be lucky to see Common Blue butterflies flitting along this gorse-lined bank.

Keep the hedge on your L as it swings L to a gate. In September you can pick Sloe berries here for wine-making or jam. Continue through the gate to a cottage ahead where you need to turn sharp R onto a hedge-lined farm-track.

Look out for Speckled Wood and Small Tortoiseshell butterflies along here.

Pass through the next gate and step into a farmyard and courtyard. Keep straight ahead along the drive as it enters a fine copper-beech hedge on both sides. Look back and you'll see the sign indicating the 3 houses that are rather pleasantly situated in this tranquil spot.

This drive which services all these houses culminates at a junction with a lane. Turn R along the lane, soon to pass Hinnington Cottages and a little further on what was once

44

Hinkesman's Hinnington Spring Brewery. Guess what? This is the very lovely and tiny wee hamlet of... Hinnington!

In a matter of yards you'll reach another charming hamlet – Grindleforge and the Oldforge bridge over Wesley Brook.

Just over the bridge look for the footpath sign on the right ③ that goes between a garage and the brook, passing a wooden bench.

You will be walking with Wesley Brook on the R all the way to Kemberton Mill, at times close to, and at others, high above it.

Continue on, entering a wonderful wood and enchanting path that climbs up and then down before exiting into a field at the stile. (Beware; the path continues but is not a right of way so keep an eye out for the stile on R – there may be a marker on a tree, there's certainly one on the stile). Climb the stile to enter the field and walk to the top right-hand corner, keeping Wesley Brook on your right, to reach another stile (ignore a make-shift stile about half-way across the field-edge over a barbed wire fence – this is not a public right of way).

Climb the stile in the corner and continue through trees, with the brook falling below you. At the next stile the path heads straight down steps into a tiny dry gorge and then just as sharply, rises up again as it passes through Kemberton Gorse. Climb a stile at the top and walk with fence on your right to another stile in the far corner. Continue straight on, still with fence on right.

As the path starts to descend you'll see another stile in front, but walk to the L of it keeping on the high ground to walk above all the trees on R to reach an external field corner at a fence to pass between an ash tree with four trunks on R and a hawthorn tree on L, to walk now with the fence on L.

A waymarker on a tree in front and the sight of another stile ahead confirm you're still on course.

Over the next stile follow the path as it passes a large holly tree on R and then descends diagonally to a kissing gate in the bottom corner. Through the gate the path passes between brook and a house.

In late summer, if the Buddleia bush is still there, you may be lucky enough to see a profusion of butterflies such as Peacock, Red Admiral, Painted Lady, Small Tortoiseshell and Comma.

Soon you'll reach a footpath signpost and our third hamlet on the walk at Kemberton Mill with the remains of an old water wheel that once powered a flour mill. Yet another charming and peaceful spot.

At the signpost take the left fork (signed Kemberton) and walk along the lane. Just past a telegraph pole take the footpath that turns acute right ④ to walk with hedge on L. As the path ends step left over a stile and into a field with a pleasantly situated bench and walk with trees on your right. You're now walking through Greenacres organic farmland.

Follow this long path until it reaches the lane, although in late summer you may want to stop at opportune moments along this grassy ride to pick some of the most delightful blackberries I've ever come across! When you reach the lane turn R and walk along it. Looking left you will see the tree-topped Lodge Hill once again, but much closer than before. This marks the final stage of the walk.

The lane goes down slightly as it bends to the right and then just before the bridge go through the metal kissing gate on your L to walk along the FP through a short wooded area.

Wesley Brook will, once more, be on your right. Amble slowly through this tiny but enchanting copse to reach another gate. Keep straight on with the brook still on your right.

Follow this well-walked path which hugs the brook through vegetation, mainly the tall pink-flowered Himalayan Balsam which proudly struts its stuff from late spring through to early autumn. This wild flower, introduced by the Victorians, is a favourite of honey bees and although somewhat invasive these days, apparently some of the finest honey is made from bees attending these flower heads. Bees are currently suffering an alarming decline as they unwittingly become host to a deadly mite along with other threats, and we all know what will happen if the busy bees all disappear; it's said we won't survive ourselves! A sobering thought. Despite the power and might of man we still rely almost entirely on the humble bumble. However, Mother nature, as always, will somehow solve the problem I'm sure.

On reaching a footbridge over the brook, cross it and follow the path into woodland. Climb George's Steps (look left to see the sign on a nearby tree) and upon reaching the top you may want to dally a while on the seat set in the most perfect position after the short toil.

You now need to summon up enough energy to tackle the final 'up' of the day; Lodge Hill - the sting in the tail. As you exit the wood at a stile just head straight up the hill on a faint path keeping close to the fence on L.

Despite the fact that Lodge Hill is a short climb there are great views back over to the Clee Hills to the south and Clent Hills to the east. On a clear day, looking south of east, you can also see the Malvern Hills in Worcestershire.

Just past the wooded hill-top look closely at the northern edge of the trees and you should be able to pick out the Ordnance Survey triangulation pillar which marks the height of this modest little hill-top at 114 mtrs (374 ft).

A little further on, look back and to the west of Lodge Hill's trees and you will see Shropshire's most prominent hill – The Wrekin.

The path continues to a stile at a gate and opens into a long straight farm track, with hedge on left and fence on right, soon changing to fence on L and hedge on R. Eventually it swings R at the bottom hedge and after a small pool on your R, deposits you on to Park Lane. Turn L and after some minutes, on reaching the junction with a main road, turn L to walk past the Park House Hotel, back to the centre of Shifnal and the Millennium Clock.

Walk 8. ✛
Picnic at Priorslee Lake - return via Kew Gardens – circular
Distance: 7 miles
Time to allow: 3½ hrs without stops
Refreshments: Pubs and tea rooms in Shifnal

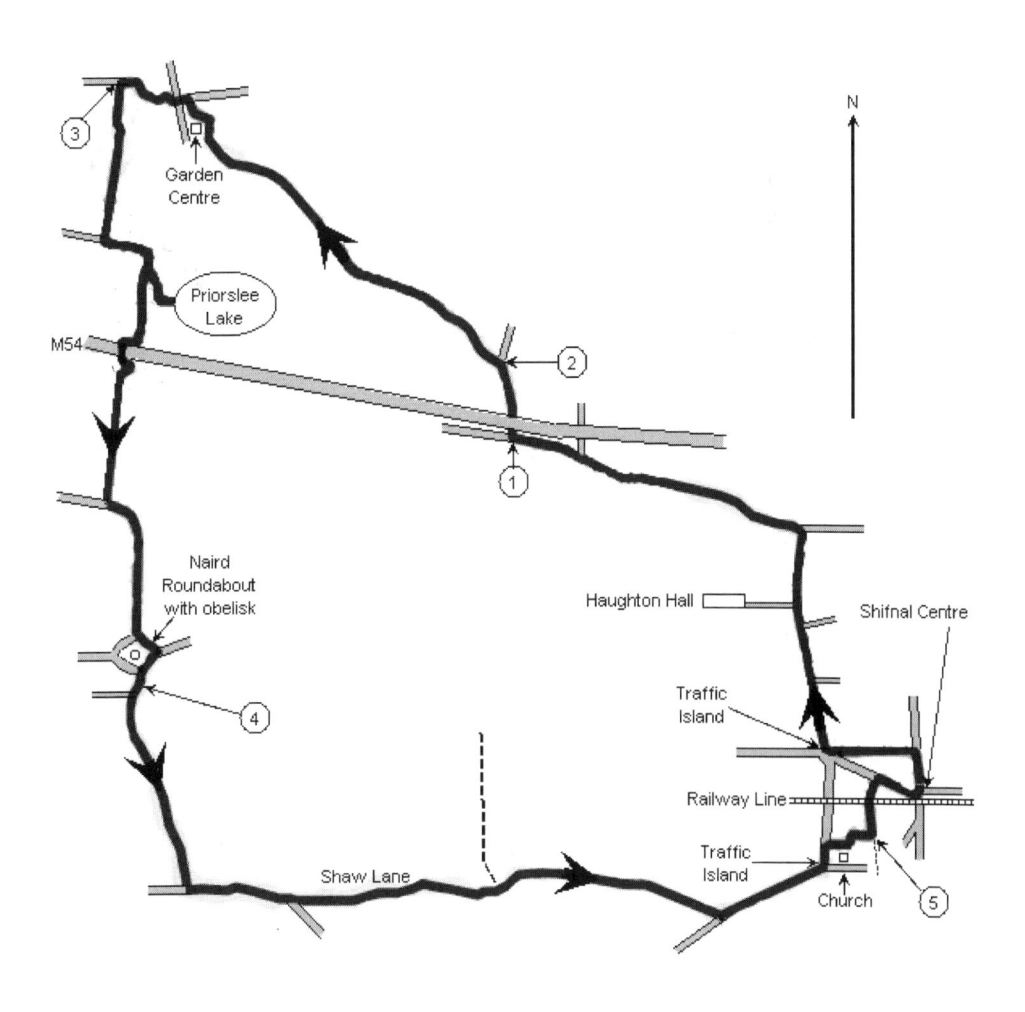

A pleasant walk along quiet rural lanes to Priorslee Lake, with ample opportunities to rest and picnic before completing the circular. The return unfortunately and unavoidably crosses the noisy M54 and then enters a trading estate, but in less than a mile it returns to tranquil country lanes.

From the Millennium Clock head north past the Co-op and turn L at the road junction to walk along Shrewsbury Road past the Medical Centre, old Fire Station (now a museum) and the old Magistrates Court.

At the traffic island turn R and walk along the very straight Haughton Lane to its end, passing Haughton Hall Hotel on the way. Turn L on reaching the road junction and walk, with great care, using the pavements until they run out, and then keeping on the right-hand side of the road so you can see oncoming traffic. Walk up this sometimes busy road for 10 minutes or so ignoring the first R turn to a farm, but taking the second one (signed Redhill) to walk along a road passing under the M54 ①.

A few minutes later take a L fork ② and walk along this narrow and quiet lane until you reach buildings in about half-an-hour.

Follow the lane as it swings L past the entrance to a garden centre on L , cross the road at the bottom and turn L to meet the main road through Priorslee. Turn R onto this road and almost immediately cross this busy main road using the pedestrian refuge and go straight ahead on to a Cycle Route (81).

At the <u>second</u> blue 'End of Cycle Route' sign turn L off here into a cul-de-sac at Cadman Drive③. Walk along, following the road which runs into Kew Gardens cul-de-sac. At the end and to the L of house No. 9, a FP on the L takes you shortly

50

through a playing field with a hard-surfaced and enclosed ball-games area.

Take the path that skirts left of this and follow with hedge on L and football field on R to a CP. Through the CP arrive at junction with a lane and footpath signs. Turn L here. On reaching gates, go through and follow the lane as it swings R. In a few yards take the lane on the L, not the FP, and you'll see Priorslee Lake ahead.

Take a path off left and find a picnic spot anywhere around here, keeping well clear of any activity with the boat club.

Marvel at the many species of bird that find this balancing lake so irresistible. In summer dragon and damselflies are also to be seen on the wing. You may even find the large caterpillars of the Drinker Moth in the grasses near the water's edge.

Return. Retrace steps along lane to just before the gated lane and this time turn L along the FP you saw earlier. Walk with fenced off area of boats on your L and eventually to a footbridge over the M54 and into Stafford Park.

For the uninitiated arriving at Stafford Park for the first time you may have conjured up a vision of beautiful parklands with herds of fallow deer, swans gliding majestically across the lake, with perhaps a stately home nestling in a pleasant dell by babbling brooks with sun-dappled woodlands to explore. Sorry but this is a trading estate! But let's put a positive spin on this;- erm... well... it doesn't take long to get through this tangle of commerce and industry, you'll soon be back into tranquillity, and the kids will love standing on the bridge watching the cars hurtling along the motorway – it's better than being at Silverstone! Does that work?

On the other side of the bridge, continue down the road past an impressive looking Chinese-style building and eventually reach a road junction. Turn L here and on reaching the busy Naird traffic-island, complete with metal obelisk, negotiate a safe way to cross straight over and onto Naird Road ④ and soon peace and quiet once more.

Walk up the hill, straight over a mini-roundabout and soon reach a lane junction. Turn L here along Shaw Lane and follow (ignoring a turn off R to the Wyke) for about 40 minutes to the main road. Turn L here for Shifnal.

On reaching the roundabout, turn L, cross the road and in a few yards turn R into the delightful Millennium Sensory Gardens, maintained entirely by local volunteers. A few happy moments can be spent here enjoying this lovely little area.

Through the other side pass by the war memorial and take a path L and then R through the churchyard. On reaching another path at the hedge turn L ⑤ to pass under the railway and in front of a neat, square house with a small bridge to its front door. This used to be the railway wash-house.

When you reach the road turn R and then next R again to walk back to your start at the Millennium Clock.

Walk 9. ✧ Nedge Hill Circular

Distance: 7.8 miles
Time to allow: 4 hrs without stops
Refreshments: Masons Arms, Kemberton (slightly off route making 8.5 miles total). Pubs and tea rooms in Shifnal

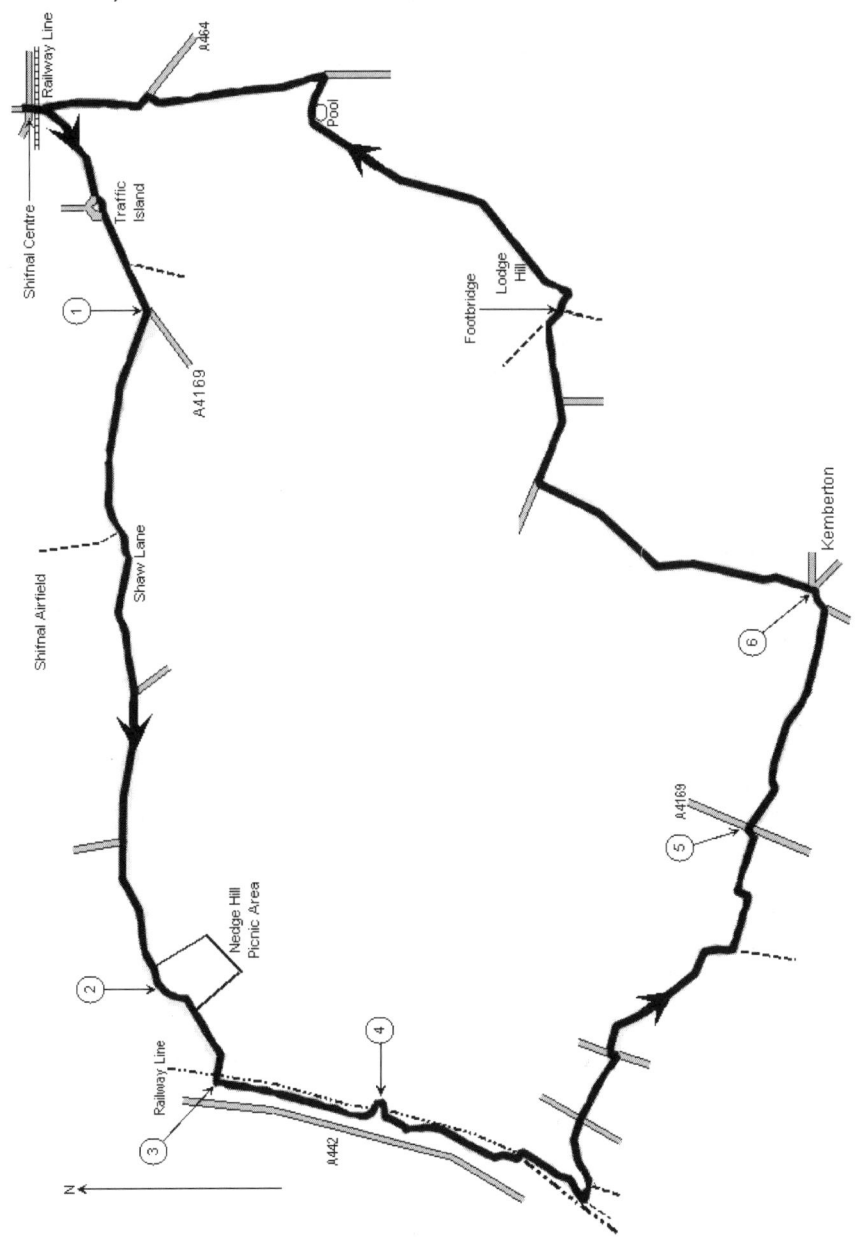

53

Not many people walk the quiet lanes to Nedge Hill from Shifnal, which is surprising given that it's a very pleasant walk. This circular includes bridleways and footpaths, with just a few stiles. All in all an enjoyable walk which few will have experienced.

Start the walk from the centre of Shifnal at the Millennium Clock and head south under the railway bridge. Opposite Odfellows Pub turn R down Church Street and follow past Old Idsall House on the R – reputed to be the oldest dwelling in Shifnal, past the church to reach a traffic island. Cross over to go along one of the main routes out of Shifnal (A4169). Continue for around 400 yards and then turn R up Shaw Lane ①, actually marked as a Quiet Lane… shhhh!

After a short while, and away from the main road, the only noise you might hear is a microlight taking-off or landing on the tiny airstrip just to the north of a FP off R. If not, then listen out for the sound of skylarks way above you.

The lane rises slowly all the way to Nedge Hill at a modest 160 metres (328'), passing Shaw Farm on the way. Ignore all turns off and keep going until you eventually reach Nedge Hill Picnic Site at woodland ②. There are fine views towards Ironbridge and Brown Clee Hill beyond.

Continue along the lane as it descends and then runs under a train line, a spur off the main Birmingham-Shrewsbury line which at the time of writing is still in use, supplying occasional shipments of coal to Ironbridge Power Station where the line ends. A few yards after passing under the bridge take the BW on the L running through trees ③.

There are parts of this track that never seem to see sunlight and it can get a little muddy, but still a nice walk, although you're now walking with the train line on your L and the very busy Eastern Primary road on your R so it's not so quiet!

In a while the path deposits you quite unceremoniously right onto a busy roundabout – Stirchley Interchange ④. Some care is needed to cross this; turn L as you reach the road and follow the barrier around, walking away from the roundabout, until the barrier ends and then cross carefully over to turn R heading back to the roundabout once more. Walk round to the L and you'll see a BW sign off L at the exit road for Bridgnorth (A442). This actually is a continuation of the BW you just left, the break in it being necessary since the building of the Eastern Primary.

Descend steeply down steps to walk alongside the train line once more. Eventually you'll reach a path junction to pass under the train line where the path swings R and follows the line now on your R. Pass a culvert on your R and after a few yards the path turns you out onto a grassy area. Turn left here and walk uphill on a well-defined path, with a wooded hillside on your R. Follow the path as it passes under a road. (This is the busy and sprawling Halesfield Industrial Estate, but fortunately the route takes you through the northern tip and back into the countryside very shortly).

So… having passed under the road continue forward through units and offices, passing soon through 2 granite boulders to climb steps to a road.

Cross over slightly to the L to pick up the BW once more. This path skirts around industrial units with woodland to L & metal fence to R. At the top of a rise the track swings R.

As you walk along there's a steady realisation that you're now escaping busy roads, industry and commerce as you head back into tranquillity that is the beautiful English countryside.

As the path narrows, follow it as it swings to R. Look out for a FP that comes off L, cross a bridge over a drainage ditch, and continue into a field to walk with hedge on your R. At the field end, turn L and then R, still with hedge on R to meet the A4169. ⑤

Cross over slightly L and take the FP through a paddock and 4 metal kissing gates. Way over to the right you should be able to pick out the distinct slope that forms Titterstone Clee Hill, with the highest hill in Shropshire Brown Clee just to its right. At the 4th gate the path turns L and then R, to rise gradually with hedge on L.

At the top the path turns R and then quickly turns L, keeping hedge on your L all the time. You'll now see Kemberton Church to your right. The path runs through 2 more metal kissing gates at a farm followed by a tree-lined tunnel and shortly after you'll reach a road at Kemberton and almost opposite is the enigmatic Kaleidoscope Theatre.

(If refreshment calls, The Masons Arms pub is just 1/3 of a mile away. Turn R to walk along the road, past the church and then R again uphill to the pub).

Turn L here and follow the road for a few yards to turn L on a FP, just past the turning for High Farm ⑥.

The path runs the gauntlet between hedges to reach a gate and then our first stile of the walk. Climb a 2nd stile to walk straight across a field to a waymarked gap in the hedge which drops through trees. When, after a few yards, you reach a field turn R to walk with trees and then hedge on your R. After 2 fields you will reach a lane where you'll turn R to walk along it as Lodge Hill rises before you.

When the lane drops downhill it turns into a wide track. Turn R at the fork and walk down this wide, often muddy track, which soon peters out to a FP near the bridge over Wesley Brook.

Cross the footbridge over the brook and follow the path into woodland. Climb George's Steps (see if you can spot the sign on a tree to your L) and upon reaching the top you may want to dally a while on the seat set in the most perfect position after the short toil.

You now need to summon up enough energy to tackle the final 'up' of the day; Lodge Hill - the sting in the tail.

As you exit the wood at a stile, just head straight up the hill on a faint path keeping close to the fence on L.

Despite the fact that Lodge Hill is a short climb there are great views back over to the Clee Hills to the south and Clent Hills to the east. On a clear day, looking south of east, you can also see the Malvern Hills in Worcestershire.

Just past the wooded hill-top look closely at the northern edge of the trees and you should be able to pick out the Ordnance Survey triangulation pillar which marks the height of this modest little hill-top at 114 mtrs (374 ft).

A little further on, look back and to the west of Lodge Hill's trees and you will see Shropshire's most prominent hill – The Wrekin.

The path continues to a stile at a gate and opens into a long straight farm track, with hedge on left and fence on right, soon changing to fence on L and hedge on R. Eventually it swings R at the bottom hedge (just over another farm-track crossing it) and after a small pool on your R, deposits you on to Park Lane. Turn L and after some minutes on reaching the junction with a main road, turn L to walk past the Park House Hotel, back to the centre of Shifnal and the Millennium Clock.

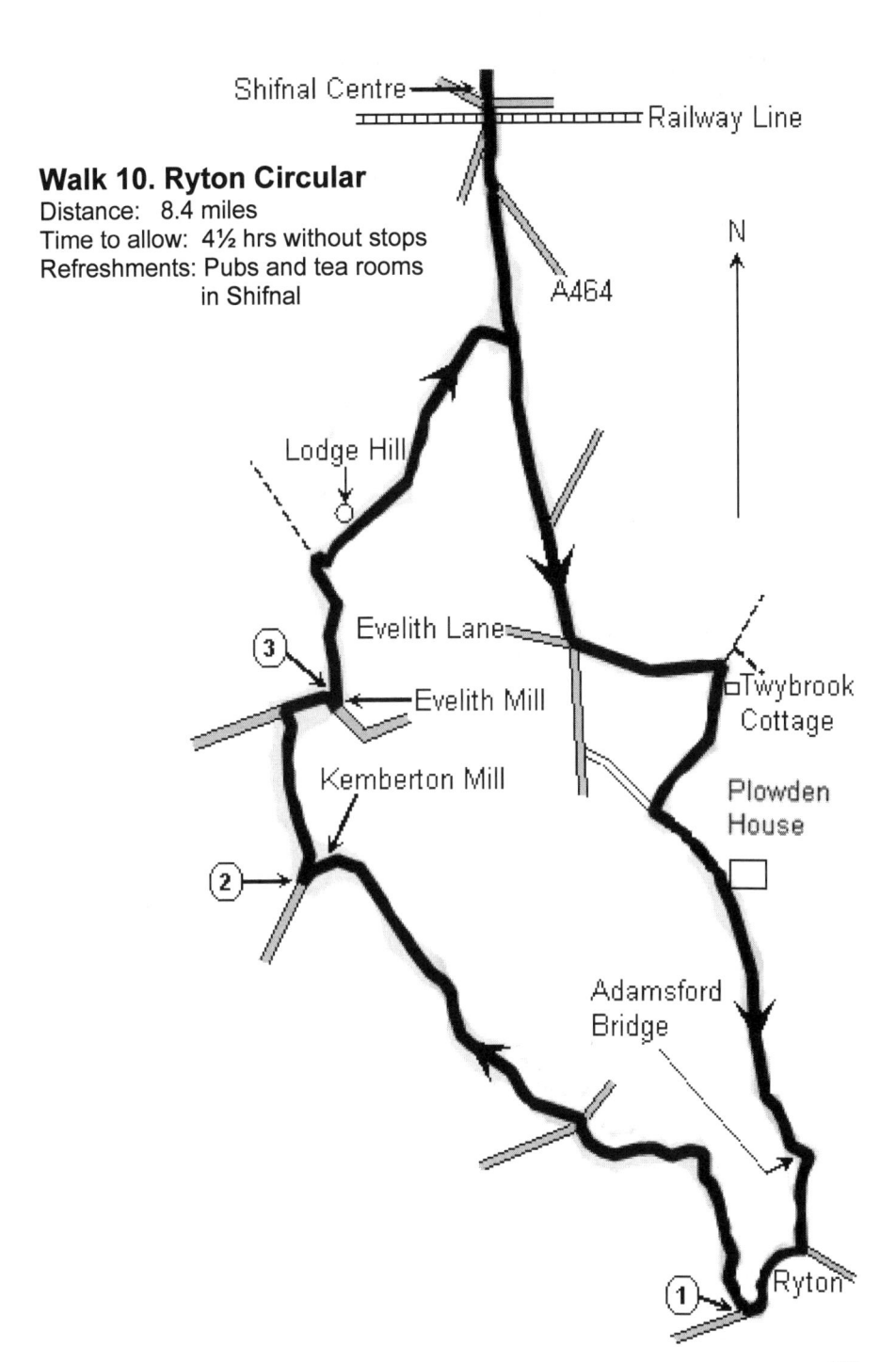

Walk 10. Ryton Circular
Distance: 8.4 miles
Time to allow: 4½ hrs without stops
Refreshments: Pubs and tea rooms
in Shifnal

*Discover the lovely countryside on Shifnal's doorstep.
The route takes in the charming hamlets of Evelith Mill,
Kemberton Mill and the tiny village of Ryton, following field
paths, quiet lanes and bridleways.*

Start the walk from the centre of Shifnal at the Millennium Clock and head south under the railway bridge, passing the Odfellows pub and the Park House Hotel. As the road bends L turn R up Park Lane (signed Ryton & Grindleforge), past St Andrews School and walk alongside a superb row of mature trees of oak, sycamore, holly, horse chestnut and beech. Soon the houses disappear as the lane narrows and becomes much quieter. Continue slightly down hill on this straight-as-a-die road until you reach Evelith Lane on the R.

Turn L here down a long drive leading to a large house (although not visible from the lane). Take the FP to the R of gate and follow it as it skirts the house and goes through a small wooded area and eventually reaches Twybrook Cottage.

Turn R here to pass in front of this lovely isolated cottage to follow a Permissive Path initially with hedge on L and once through a gate, follow with hedge on R. In a few short minutes arrive at another drive. Turn L here to pass by Plowden House (built 1764 on the site of the original Hatton Grange).

Behind the house is woodland and host to a series of small but oddly named lagoons which can be seen on the OS map; Purgatory Pool, Abbot's Pool, Hell Pool and Bath Pool. Intriguing though they may be, they're all out of bounds and out of sight to the public.

Follow the farm track for a further 20 minutes or so and cross what is known as Adamsford Bridge (but not marked) over the River Worfe. Just after (and ignoring a makeshift style over barbed wire) take a sharp R at a hedge and follow the track which turns into a delightful sunken path. On emerging go through the gate and follow the FP to the lane at Ryton. Turn R here to walk past the church and descend to a crossroads where you turn R. A few yards over the bridge, look for a gate and stile on your R. ① This is a Permissive Path which follows the charming Wesley Brook on the R to the sleepy hamlet of Grindleforge. Keep the brook on your R all the time through fields, ignoring a footbridge over the water, until you see a stile just to the L of the brook near a lane bridge and cottages.

Climb the stile and cross over the lane to the R to pick up the FP between a garage and Wesley Brook at the side of the terraced houses. There's a seat here by the water and makes for a useful stop.

Continue on along an enchanting path, through wonderful woodland that climbs up and then down before exiting R into a meadow at a stile. Head across the field to another stile near the top right-hand corner, keeping Wesley Brook on your right (ignore a make-shift stile about half-way across the field over a barbed wire fence – this is not a public right of way). Continue through trees with the brook falling below you. The path heads straight down the steps and then just as sharply rises up again as it passes through Kemberton Gorse.

Climb a stile at the top and walk with hedge on your R to another stile in the far corner. Continue straight on, over stile, keeping hedge on R.

The path soon drops slightly under a hawthorn tree at a fence and then goes uphill again, keeping the tree-line on your right.

This is a favourite spot of mine on the walk where many a pleasant half-hour or more has been spent in quiet

61

ponderance. In the summer, you might see a dragonfly or two here.

Continue on the same line to reach a fence where you walk between an ash tree and a hawthorn, keeping the fence on your left as you pass through them.

Cross a stile and walk forward a few yards keeping L of a large holly tree. From here follow the path that goes diagonally down to a gate in the bottom right-hand corner where you meet up once more with Wesley Brook. This is another charming and peaceful hamlet, Kemberton mill. The path then passes in front of a cottage with Kemberton Mill Cottage towering behind.

In the late summer look out for butterflies such as Peacock, Red Admiral, Comma and Small Tortoiseshell nectaring on a large Buddleia bush.

As you pass the bottom cottage take the left fork (signed Kemberton) and walk along the lane. Just past a telegraph pole take the footpath that turns acute right with a hedge on your left. ②. As the path ends, step left over a stile and into a field with a pleasantly situated bench and walk with trees on your right.

Follow this long path until it reaches a slightly awkward stile on to the lane although, in late summer, you may want to stop at opportune moments along this grassy ride to pick some of the most delightful blackberries I've ever come across!

When you reach the lane turn R. As you walk along the lane you will see the tree-topped Lodge Hill to your L once again but much closer than before. This marks the final stage of the walk.

The lane goes down slightly as it bends to the right and then just before the bridge go through the kissing gate on your L ③ to walk along the FP through a short wooded area.. Wesley Brook will, once more, be on your R. Amble slowly through this tiny but enchanting copse to reach another gate. Keep straight on with the brook still on your R.

Follow this path which hugs the brook through vegetation, mainly the tall pink-flowered Himalayan Balsam proudly strutting its stuff from late spring through to early autumn.

This non-native wild flower, introduced by the Victorians, is a favourite of honey bees and although somewhat invasive these days, apparently some of the finest honey is made from bees attending these flower heads. Our bees are currently suffering an alarming decline, due to several threats including unwittingly becoming host to a deadly mite, but mother nature, will somehow solve the problem I'm sure. It is a sobering thought though, that if all the busy bees were to disappear – we'd struggle to survive ourselves! Despite the power and might of man we still rely so heavily on the humble bumble.

On reaching a footbridge over the brook cross it and follow the path into woodland. Climb George's Steps (see if you can spot the sign on a tree to your L) and upon reaching the top you may want to dally a while on the seat set in the most perfect position after the short toil.

You now need to summon up enough energy to tackle the final 'up' of the day; Lodge Hill - the sting in the tail.

As you exit the wood at a stile just head straight up the hill on a faint path keeping close to the fence on L.

Despite the fact that Lodge Hill is a short climb there are great views back over to the Clee Hills to the south and Clent Hills to the east. On a clear day, looking south of east, you can also see the Malvern Hills in Worcestershire.

Just past the wooded hill-top look closely at the northern edge of the trees and you should be able to pick out the Ordnance Survey triangulation pillar which marks the height of this modest little hill-top at 114 mtrs (374 ft).

A little further on, look back and to the west of Lodge Hill's trees and you will see Shropshire's most prominent hill – The Wrekin.

The path continues to a stile at a gate and opens into a long straight farm track, with hedge on left and fence on right, soon changing to fence on L and hedge on R. Eventually it swings R at the bottom hedge (just over another farm-track crossing it) and after a small pool on your R, deposits you on to Park Lane. Turn L and after some minutes on reaching the junction with a main road, turn L to walk past the Park House Hotel, back to the centre of Shifnal and the Millennium Clock.

Walk 11. Lizard Wood Circular
Distance: 8.9 miles
Time to allow: 4½ hrs without stops
Refreshments: Pubs and tea rooms in Shifnal

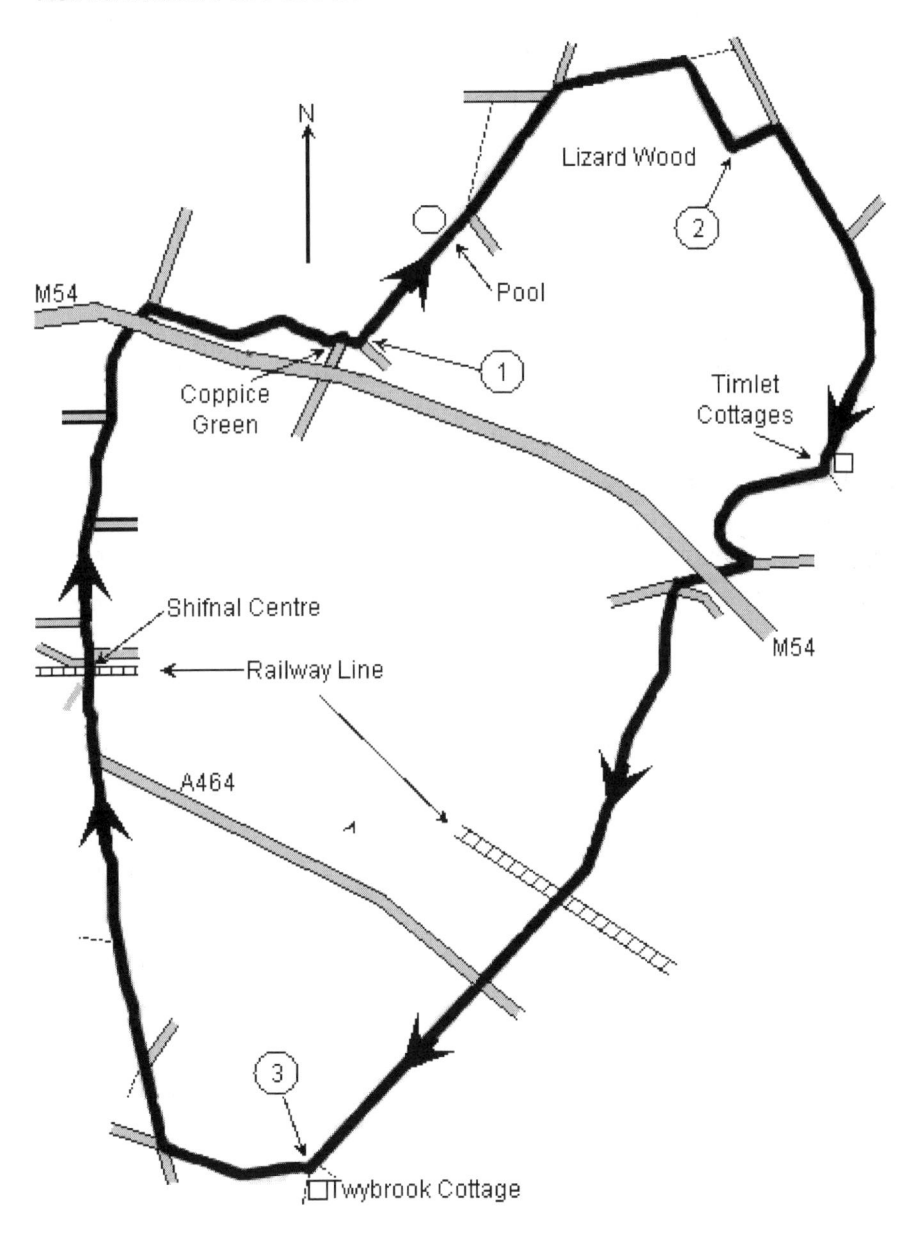

65

Lizard Wood is a privately owned large wood/small forest with no public access but this splendid walk along paths, bridleways and quiet country lanes skirts about half of this large woodland. That's not all that's great about this walk though, but you'll have to do it to find out!

Start the walk from the centre of Shifnal at the Millennium Clock and head north along Cheapside and High Street passing the Co-op on your R and past all the shops, restaurants, library and all the pubs (Royal George being the last one) to leave Shifnal behind. As you pass under M54 bridge take the FP on your right. This runs alongside the motorway for a while and you'll probably scare up pheasants in the hedgerow and spot squirrels in the trees. They all seem totally oblivious to the roar of the traffic.

Soon our path drifts away from the noise and crosses a brook over a footbridge where you turn left to follow the hedge on your left. Pass through a fence with pond on R where the path turns R.

Cross the drive to Coppice Green House and go over the stile at the side of the gates. Walk diagonally across this small grassy area and onto the lane.

①Turn L along the lane and in a few yards take the FP on L.

Follow the obvious path across the field to yonder hedge and gap at telegraph pole. Continue straight ahead through the next field. Lizard Wood is ahead. We will shortly be walking along the other side of this large wood. Go through a third hedge and head downhill to a small fishing lake.

Exit onto the lane and turn L to walk up this delightful oak tree-lined avenue – this is Coppice Green Lane and you'll soon be walking alongside the western edge of Lizard Wood on your R.

On reaching a lane junction turn R and then just as the lane bends L, just after the private entrance to woods, take the FP on your right to walk alongside the northern edge of Lizard Wood to the field corner where you turn R still hugging the edge of the wood now on its eastern side.

②At the next field corner turn L and at the bottom you will alight onto Lizard Lane. Turn R and walk along this quiet lane for about a mile-and-a-half, ignoring turns to L and R, and eventually meet the busy Tong - Shifnal road. Turn right here under the M54 once again and in a short while (just past the Neachley Lane turn) leave the traffic noise behind as you follow the Monarch's Way FP on L.

Another peaceful and tranquil stroll rich in flora and fauna. The Wrekin will come into view on your right.

Eventually pass over Bonemill Bridge (unmarked) which crosses the Birmingham – Shrewsbury railway line. Look back and view the large expanse of trees that is Lizard Wood.

Go past a few cottages to reach the A464. Carefully cross straight over here and continue along the Monarch's Way.

③When you reach the isolated Twybrook Cottage turn R along a FP through trees and alongside a large garden belonging to an equally large house. The path then leads onto the house's drive by a posh gate where you turn L and walk along it away from the house and in a few minutes arrive at Hinnington Road.

Turn R and walk up this long straight lane and in around a mile-and-a-quarter you will meet houses and your return to Shifnal. On reaching the main road simply turn L and walk back to the town centre.

Walk 12. The Bell at Tong Circular
Distance: 9.8 miles
Time to allow: 5 hrs without stops
Refreshments: The Bell Inn at Tong.
                   Pubs and tea rooms in Shifnal

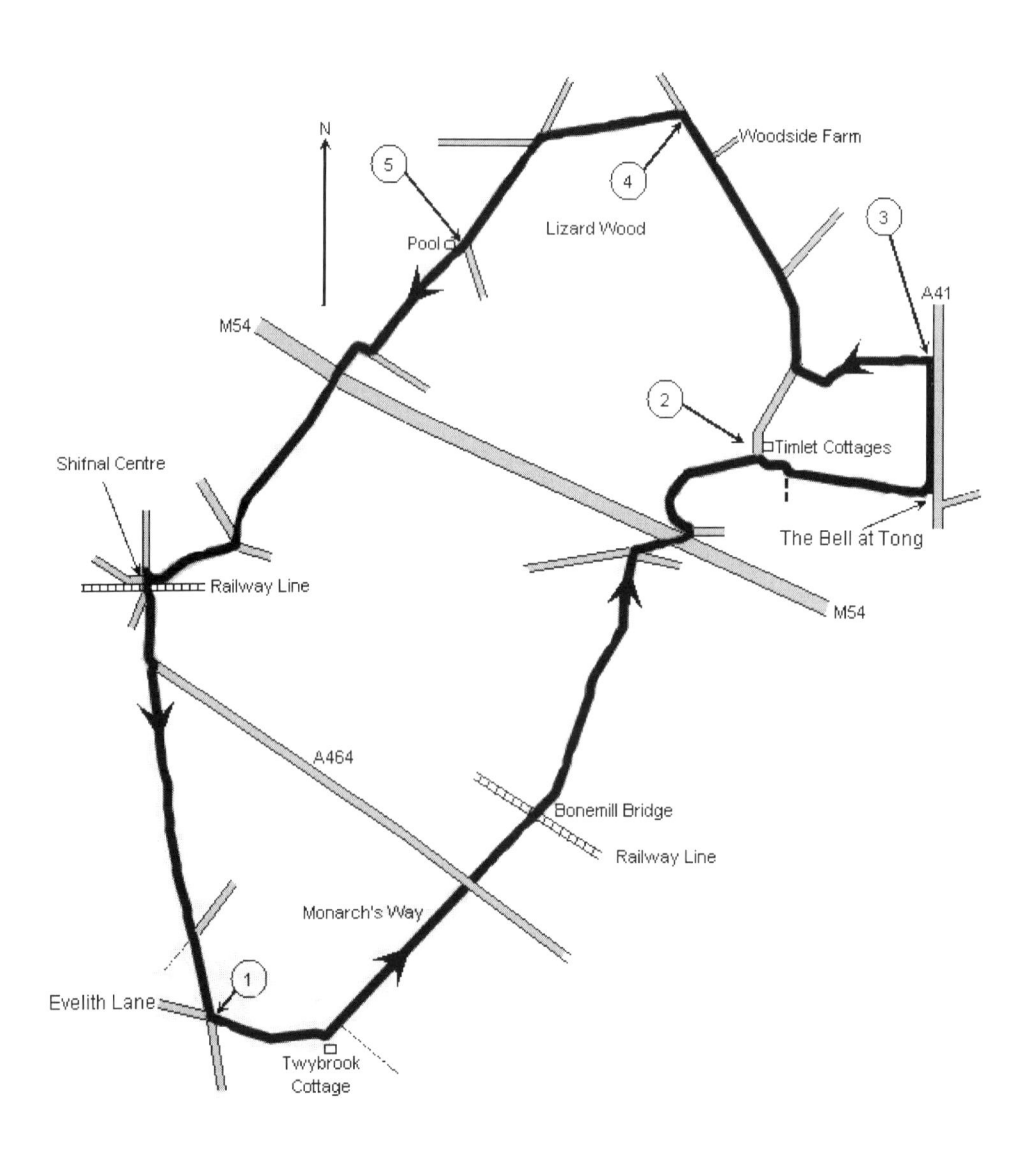

68

This delightful walk heads over to the village of Tong with an optional stop-over at The Bell Inn for lunch - and why not? The return includes a trip down a little-known, almost secret, wooded gorge and then through an ancient sunken path.

Start the walk from the centre of Shifnal at the Millennium Clock and head south under the railway bridge, passing the Odfellows pub and the Park House Hotel. As the road bends L turn R up Park Lane (signed Ryton & Grindleforge), past St Andrews School and walk alongside a superb row of mature trees of oak, sycamore, holly, horse chestnut and beech. Soon the houses disappear as the lane narrows and becomes much quieter. Continue slightly down hill on this straight-as-a-die road until you reach a lane coming off on the R which is Evelith Lane.

① Turn L here along the drive to the gate of a house with hedge on R. *(This is part of The Monarch's Way - a 615 mile National Trail and in fact this will take you all the way to The Bell Inn at Tong).*

At the gate a FP goes to the R and then L as it skirts the house, through a small wooded area and eventually reaches Twybrook Cottage. Turn L here along this wide and peaceful track for 2 miles, crossing the A464 and some time after the Birmingham-Shrewsbury railway line at the unmarked Bonemill Bridge.

Keep following the main drive past 2 houses on R. Just past the second house there's a gate which may be closed displaying a 'Private Drive' sign, ignore the sign and go through the gate – this is a public right of way, and confirmed by a Monarch's Way marker on the right-hand post. Continue on this wide drive with hedge on R and in a few yards enter a wooded area, eventually arriving at another main road near Neachley Lane.

Cross this often fast and busy road and walk R to pass under the M54. Just after turn L along a much quieter road past Lizard House and some time later when you reach a sharp left at Timlet Cottages, turn R down a wide BW between 2 white posts. ②

Pass a house with pool on L and another pool through the hedge on R. When you reach another house with a drive, turn L to walk uphill parallel to the drive and into a field. Keep walking in the same direction, keeping the hedge on R until you reach the main A41 road. Turn R here and in a few yards past the petrol station you will arrive at The Bell Inn for a pint and a bite.

Return via A41 to the point where you arrived at this trunk road, but instead of retracing steps along the FP turn R to walk with the hedge on your R parallel to the A41. This is a Permissive Path opened up under The Countryside Stewardship Scheme and forms a convenient start to the route back to Shifnal.

Count the fields as you walk. Half way through the third field with gate on R, turn L along a wide track leading to trees ③. As soon as the track swings to L, immediately leave the track by turning R to walk with a grassy field boundary on R which soon becomes a ditch and heads towards a tree-line. Follow trees on R where the ditch slowly forms a deep, wooded gorge and stream which will shortly be crossed.

As gorge and tree-line swing slightly to the L look for a post and marker for a FP which takes you R downhill through this delightful tiny woodland to a footbridge across the stream. On the other side keep in same direction and head through a sunken path. Soon, a stile drops you on to Lizard Lane. Turn R and walk along this long straight lane for half-an-hour or so.

A few yards past the entrance to Woodside Farm on your R turn L up a Restricted Bridleway. ④. This is a wide grassy track with hedge on R. Keep straight on at a marker post and at the next marker the track goes R and then L to walk with a line of ancient oak trees on your L. As you near the hedge-line ahead, aim for the top L corner to the wood between 2 boulders and arrive at a lane. Turn L here passing the entrance (private estate) to Lizard Wood and then take the L turn onto Coppice Green Lane (signed Stanton 1½).

Walk down this long, straight, but very pleasant, tree-lined lane until reaching a left-hand bend ⑤ and then continue in the same direction on a FP slightly uphill by a small fishing pool.

When you reach Coppice Green Lane again, turn R and follow it all the way passing Idsall School on the R and Aston Lodge on L to meet another road. Turn L, then immediate R and in a few minutes you'll arrive at Shifnal's Millennium Clock and the end of your walk.

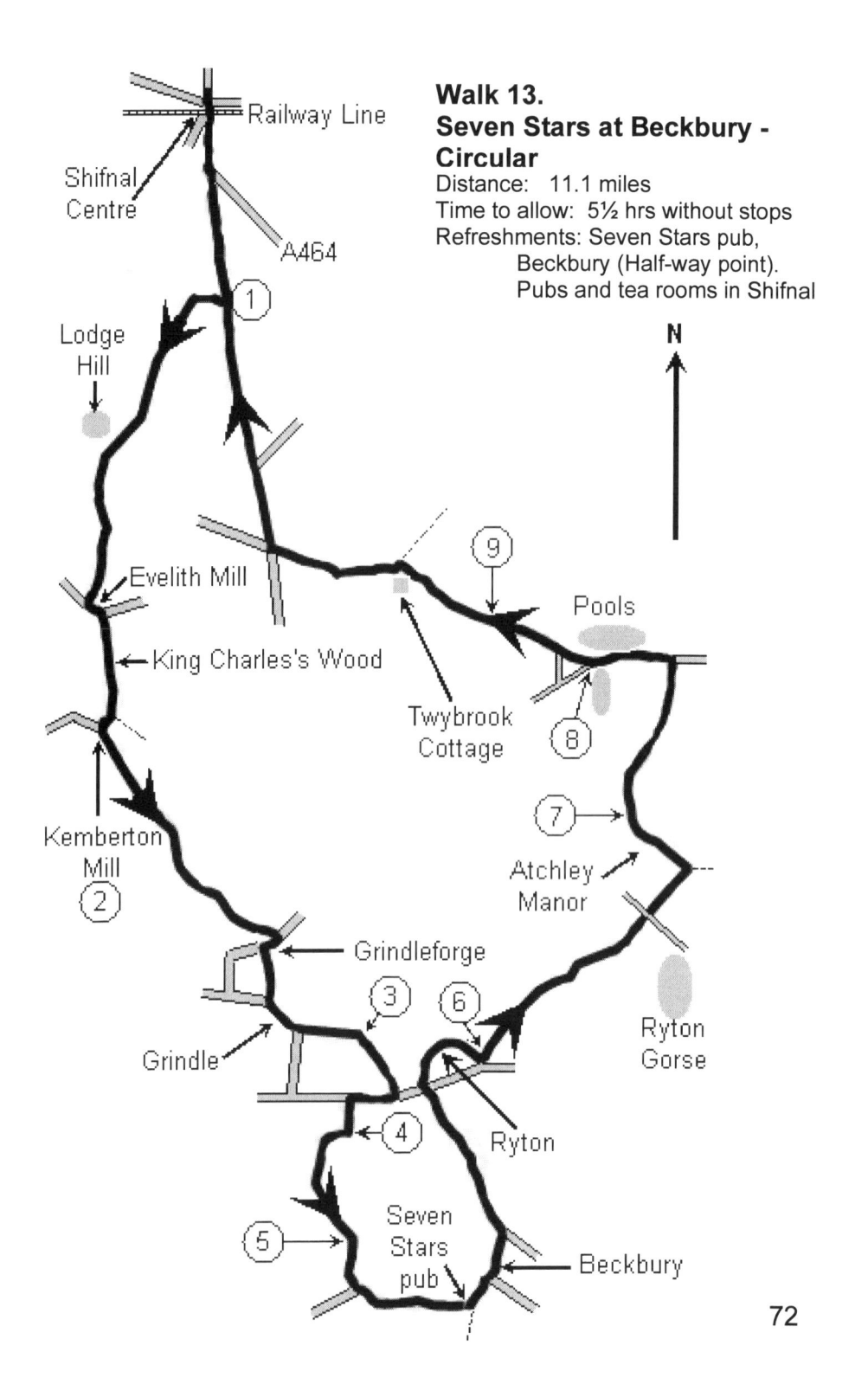

Walk 13.
Seven Stars at Beckbury - Circular
Distance: 11.1 miles
Time to allow: 5½ hrs without stops
Refreshments: Seven Stars pub, Beckbury (Half-way point). Pubs and tea rooms in Shifnal

A really super circular exploring the best of what the paths south of Shifnal have to offer, with lovely views coupled with changing terrain and aspect. Particularly enjoyable on a nice warm day with the delightful Seven Stars pub at the half-way mark! Perfect! Definitely one of my all-time favourite Shifnal walks.

Start the walk from the centre of Shifnal at the Millennium Clock and head south under the railway bridge, passing the Odfellows pub and the Park House Hotel. As the road bends L turn R up Park Lane (signed Ryton & Grindleforge), past St Andrews School to walk alongside a superb row of mature trees of oak, sycamore, holly, horse chestnut and beech.

A few minutes past the turning for Lodge Hill Farm take the FP on the R ① past a bungalow, over a stile and on to a wide track with pool on L. The track soon bends sharply L and heads slightly uphill with a hedge on L and fence on R. Then as it bends slightly left it changes to hedge now on R and fence on L. Go through a gate or climb the stile to walk with fence on R (you will see The Wrekin in the distance, in front and to your R) to the top of Lodge Hill.

You will have hardly noticed the climb but in a short while you'll be at the top with a wonderful vista for your eyes to feast upon.

Ahead you'll see Shropshire's highest hill, Brown Clee complete with masts and to its L Titterstone Clee (Shropshire's third highest hill) which has an Earth Satellite in the shape of a golf ball near its summit. On a clear day you can see The Malvern Hills ahead and to the L. Looking straight ahead you will see a tall chimney – this is Ironbridge Power Station with its cooling towers just out of sight sitting in Ironbridge Gorge. The woodland of Benthall Edge is also visible behind and to the L of the chimney.

As you descend leave the fence by taking the faint path off L and head down hill to a stile (at the right hand end of the line of oak trees) and into the farmyard. Continue ahead with conifer hedge on R and arrive at a drive to the farmhouse. Keep walking in the same direction along the drive and immediately past the bungalow on R, climb the stile into a field and a 2nd stile a few yards away into woodland. Follow this path as it descends and passes a Hansel & Gretel type cottage.

Over the stile at the bottom turn L, then in a few yards R, then L again and through the large gate in front, with the cottage now behind you, to arrive at a lane. Turn L to walk along the lane in front of an imposing looking building on your L - *Evelith Mill (built 1847) - with the remains of what used to be a water wheel and flour mill powered by Wesley Brook which must have been a great deal deeper, wider and faster than it is today.*

In a few yards take the bridleway on the R through woodland. This is King Charles's Wood *so named as part of the route taken by King Charles II after he fled north, then east and finally way down south to Brighton and over to France following his defeat in the Battle of Worcester at Powick Bridge. This forms a tiny part of the 615 mile National Trail – The Monarch's Way.*

Depending upon the time of year you may see squirrels and pheasants, along with the call of the Buzzard overhead. On a hot summer's day you enter this superb woodland to a refreshingly cool atmosphere dappled by sunlight as the rays streak through the foliage.

At the end of the wood turn R at a path junction, over 2 footbridges and weir, passing tumble-down buildings on the R, through a gate and onto a lane at the delightful hamlet of Kemberton Mill and the site of yet another flour mill.

❷ Turn L here (marked Grindleforge on finger-sign post) to pass in front of a house on R. On this stretch you will be walking with Wesley Brook on the L all the way to Grindleforge, at times close to, and at others high above it.

Beyond the house, go through the kissing gate and follow the path diagonally uphill, passing to the R of a large holly tree and then a stile beyond.

Over the stile follow the path with fence on R and a nice view of Wesley Brook below to L. Shortly you will pass between an ash tree with 4 trunks and a hawthorn tree at a fence corner and continue in the same direction, keeping above the trees on your L, to reach a fence and walk with it on your L.

Climb the next stile with fence and brook still on L. Climb another stile to descend steps into a tiny dry gorge known as Kemberton Gorse and climb up steps the other side. Climb 2 more stiles to reach a large field and walk downhill keeping fence and brook on L. Ignore a path on L which is not a public right of way and eventually reach the tapered corner of this field where it meets the brook. Climb the stile into a lovely bit of woodland and turn L to follow the path as it rises and dips to reach the lane at the tiny hamlet of Grindleforge.

Turn R to walk up the lane passing houses on R. As you reach the last house look L for a FP opposite the holly hedge, about halfway along. Climb the stile and head uphill with hedge on R. The large white building you see in front and to the left as you commence a slight descent is in Ryton.

Once over the next 2 stiles (which can be a little overgrown in summer but it's only a few yards) you'll arrive at a lane in another hamlet; this is Grindle. Turn R and then immediate L to walk along the lane with houses on L. Just past the last house take the FP on L to walk through a large field with hedge on R. As you approach the next stile Ryton church appears in front of you, over the other side of a small valley.

③Climb the stile and turn R to walk with hedge on R and in a few yards leave the hedge to descend slightly and head for the bottom corner of the trees in front, to walk below them to an awkward fence and wooden gate at a house and buildings. A short path then deposits you at the lane and an old phone box on the edge of Ryton.

Turn R to walk up the lane. As it levels out turn L to walk a wide straight farm track with a metal gate at the end. Through the gate, stop and take stock: ④ Look half-right and through a large gap in the trees you should be able to see a stile in the hedge beyond, but because there's a valley between you and the stile you need to turn R and walk with hedge on R cutting across the corner to reach said stile. This is the head of a lovely valley that looks down towards Beckbury and our half-way point.

Over the stile turn L to walk with hedge now on L. As the fence turns to the R climb the stile that comes into view and turn R with fence now on R. ⑤ On reaching the trees turn L to head downhill, still keeping fence and now trees on R. Wesley Brook is still to be seen in the valley below. At the bottom of the trees turn R to follow the line of the fence and at a marker head towards a footbridge crossing a stream. This is Mad Brook.

Another footbridge takes you over what is quite often marshy ground. Turn slightly L and walk slightly uphill towards a house and stile to lane. Turn L to walk along the lane and in a few minutes arrive at the Seven Stars pub at Beckbury. The ramblers entrance is round to the left, the second door leads into the bar (first door is the restaurant).

Return: Standing on the lane with the pub behind you turn L to walk up the lane into Beckbury. Just past a sharp right-hand bend take the farm track off L, there's a waymarker on the metal gate post and a further waymarker on a wooden post a few yards further on as a confirmer. Go through a kissing gate to walk with allotment on R and then gardens backing on to houses. The path ends, as the houses do, at a short surfaced track leading down to the lane. This area is known as The Hern.

Turn L past a house called Greystones to walk down the lane passing Denton Pool on the R and in about 15 minutes arrive at Ryton.

As you reach a junction with another lane, cross straight over to walk up hill on a wide, rough lane, to reach the church at the top where the track becomes a surfaced lane.

Continue to a junction with another lane and turn L. In about 20 yards ⑥ turn L at a house (East Lea) to walk along a farm track, between a wall on the L and hedge on R, to a gate. Go through and continue on this wide farm track. After about 15 minutes the track meets a junction with a lane. Turn R and then immediate L through double gates and follow the FP with hedge on L. The wood across the field to your R is Ryton Gorse.

On reaching double gates again, go through and turn L to follow another wide farm track to walk with hedge and fence on L and soon farm buildings on L.

Looking left approaching the farm buildings you will see, once more, Titterstone Clee Hill and to its right; Shropshire's highest - Brown Clee Hill at 1772' (540m).

When the concrete farm track ends continue in the same direction on a grassy track which, in a few yards, heads R downhill through trees on a FP. At the bottom, follow as it swings to the R, and in a few yards turn L to cross a footbridge over a stream which in fact is the River Worfe.

⑦ Through the gate on the other side continue in the same direction for a few yards and then err slightly to the R, going slightly uphill to a white marker post at trees ahead. Continue up the grassy track on L, through a small wooded area, to another white marker post and stile which deposits you into a field.

The path now goes diagonally R aiming for a lone tree with buildings in the distance behind it, but if the field is ploughed or heavily cropped with no obvious path, follow the field boundary starting with the woodland on your R to reach the lone tree and another marker post. Follow the wide farm track with hedge on R and as you look right you'll see the silver, flat-topped building housing RAF Cosford's Cold War Museum.

Soon you will reach the farm buildings which will be on your R to a lane. Turn L along the lane to walk past a pair of houses on your R.

After a short distance you'll pass a pool on your R and then another on the L. As the right-hand pool ends ⑧ turn R off the lane just past a small brick-built building, onto a wide FP to walk with hedge and trees on R. Continue in same direction to another white marker post to reach a lane at a bend. Walk along the lane continuing in the same direction (i.e. don't turn L) with a house and sheds across a field to your R and shortly pass an isolated house on L. On reaching a junction with another lane at the house, continue straight over to a wide farm track with small wooded areas on both sides.

When the wood on your R ends in a few yards continue in same direction to reach the end of the wood on L at a white marker post. ⑨ Continue straight across the large field ahead in the same direction – there is often a tractor track to follow – to reach trees on the other side. As you get close to the other side of the field you'll see another white marker post confirming the route.

Continue in the same direction with small copse and stream to L. On reaching a lane turn L and in a few yards turn R, just before Twybrook Cottage and follow the FP as it skirts the grounds of a large house. Soon the gate to the house is reached where you turn L to walk along its drive, leaving the house behind you.

When you reach a lane (with Evelith Lane straight across) turn R to walk for around 30 mins up this long lane which then descends slightly, with views through the hedge on your left to The Wrekin and eventually the welcoming sight of St Andrews Church in Shifnal will come into view in front. You are now on the road that you left Shifnal on some hours ago. Arriving at the junction with the main road a L turn will take you, in just a few more minutes, back to the centre of Shifnal and your start point at the Millennium Clock.

Walk 14. ✧ Granville Nature Reserve – circular or linear– you choose!

Circular: Distance: 11.7 miles
　　　　Time to allow: 6 hrs without stops
　　　　Refreshments: Suggest picnic lunch on arrival at the reserve.
　　　　　　　Pubs and tea rooms in Shifnal
Linear: Distance: 6.8
　　　　Time to allow: 3¾ hrs without stops
　　　　Transport: 2 cars, taxi or bus from Asda for return
　　　　Refreshments: Suggest picnic lunch on arrival at the reserve.

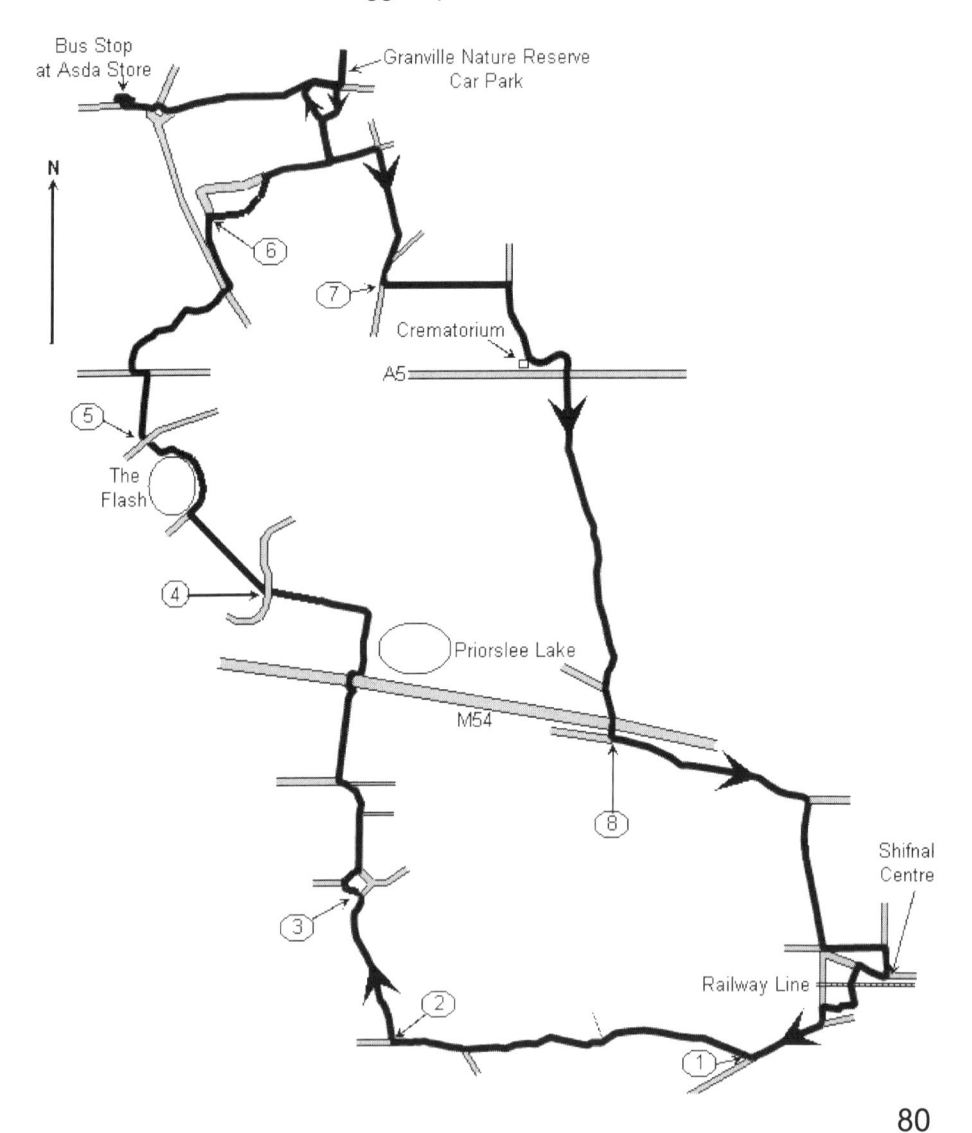

This is an excellent 6.8 miles route from Shifnal to Granville Nature Reserve taking in the source of Wesley Brook at The Flash. Not too long after you will reach delightful Granville Nature Reserve which is just such a lovely setting for a picnic – wonderful views from the 'The Top of the World' and surrounded by nature at its best.

There are then three distinct alternatives for returning to Shifnal:-

1) *Car. With 2 cars available leave a car at the Granville Nature Reserve car park to drive back*

2) *Bus. Exit the Granville Nature Reserve car park at the main gate and turn R to walk along the lane for about 20 minutes to the roundabout, cross over and pick up a bus to Telford at the Asda store. From here another bus will take you back to Shifnal (check timetables beforehand).*

3) *Walk. Turn this linear walk into a circular – you're over half way at this point – it's just 4.9 miles (about 2½ hrs) back to Shifnal.*

NB: This walk has been given the ✧ symbol as there are a couple of unavoidable but short sections, of just a few minutes, through housing estates and a trading estate but this should not detract from an otherwise splendid walk.

Start the walk from the centre of Shifnal at the Millennium Clock with your back to Katrina's Card Shop, and head R to the pedestrian crossing and walk under the railway bridge.

Opposite Odfellows Pub turn R down Church Street and walk past Old Idsall House on the R – reputed to be the oldest dwelling in Shifnal, past the church to reach a traffic island. Cross over to go along one of the main routes out of Shifnal (A4169) heading towards Ironbridge. Continue for around 400 yards and then turn R up Shaw Lane ①, actually marked as a Quiet Lane… shhhh!

After a short while, and away from the main road, the only noise you might hear is a microlight taking-off or landing on the tiny airstrip nearby. If not, then listen out for the sound of skylarks way above you.

The lane rises slowly for 1.25 miles (approx 30 mins) passing Shaw Farm on the way. Ignoring a lane on R marked Castle Cats on the nearby telegraph pole and a L turn signed The Wyke, eventually reach a sign indicating Naird Lane. ②

Turn R to walk along it soon passing over a traffic Island and arrive at a larger island – Naird Roundabout – with a striking obelisk in the centre. ③ You will need to cross carefully to the road directly opposite, (there is a pedestrian path to the L of the roundabout) to enter Stafford Park Industrial Estate. Don't worry you're only here for a few minutes!

Over the railway line take the 3rd road on R - Stafford Park 6 - and walk along to its end where you'll pass an impressive looking Chinese-type building (actually a Taiwanese Pagoda built for an IT company). Just past here turn R and then take the FP almost immediately on L which will take you over the M54 on a footbridge.

Over the motorway turn R and follow the FP as it heads towards Priorslee Lake. If you want to explore the lake walk past the boat enclosure on your R and when you reach a FP sign turn acute R to follow a concrete road leading to the lake. If you're not visiting the lake continue straight on at the sign as the FP turns into a road, swinging L to gates.

Go through and walk straight on along the road using the adjacent path which moves from R of road to L with a ditch on L carrying Wesley Brook – the source of which is another body of water you will soon meet – The Flash.

Wesley Brook starts at The Flash, flows through Shifnal before converging with the River Worfe near Ryton and then joins the River Severn near Bridgnorth, eventually disgorging into the Atlantic Sea via the Bristol Channel.

After reaching houses on your right, the path soon veers off L to pass under a road ④. At a path junction with a pool on R turn R. Follow the path as it twists and turns. After another pool on L continue straight on at crossroads of paths. Shortly you will walk with school on L.

Keep on the same path ignoring all paths off. On reaching a path junction turn R and shortly walk with small woodland on R and bank on L with Wesley Brook on L. At the top of a short rise you will reach The Flash at a path junction at a 'Beware open water nearby' sign. Turn R to skirt this lovely and popular lake. The route goes right round to the far side soon crossing over 2 foot bridges - ignore all paths off R.

Eventually on reaching the other side at a 'Danger No Swimming' sign take the path R to head towards a main road but the path actually goes underneath it through another tunnel. ⑤ Through the tunnel turn R up steps and continue along the road ahead between houses soon passing London Road on the L to continue forward and up the hill. This is Ashley Road. Continue on going straight over a crossroads to continue uphill now on Snow Hill.

Arriving at a road junction at the top turn L (St. Georges Church is across and to the right). In a short while just before a pub (Cottage Spring) turn R down Duke Street, which starts as a wide track and then narrows to a FP skirting a heather-clad hillside - an old pit mound. At the top of a short rise go through a gate and as you look over the new Redhill housing estate, you will see Lilleshall Hill in the middle distance, resplendent with its monument atop.

Turn R here and then at a path junction turn L to walk with school playing field on R. Climb steps and descend steps to a footbridge crossing the busy Redhill Way road. The path swings L at the other side and turns into a lane. As it reaches another parallel lane, cross to walk on this and in about 140 paces (at the time of writing there is a tyre serving as a marker), take the tiny FP off R ❻ heading more-or-less in the same direction (ignore an almost immediate path on R) to enter woodland which is part of the Granville Nature Reserve.

Soon the path meets a wider path at a red marker 'Granville Heritage Trail' (when you arrive at the car park notice board, for future reference take a leaflet detailing this excellent walk which features the industrial heritage of the area). Turn R at this marker and continue, ignoring a path off R where soon this now wider path exits woodland to reach grassland on the L. Continue straight on until you reach a FP on L going off at right-angles to walk with a fence and enclosed horse track on your R. This path skirts a pool on the L, ignore a R path, and soon reach another pool on your R.

This area was once a hive of activity with the nearby Old Lodge Furnaces (which can be visited by taking a path off left). The pool that you have arrived at was an essential part of the industry and was originally connected to the Donnington Wood Tub Boat Canal.

Continue along the path to reach a gate leading to a lane. Turn R and in a few minutes turn L into the Granville Nature Reserve car park. Picnic suggestion; walk right through the car park and up the steps at the far side to reach a wide area known locally as 'The Top of The World' with fine views west and north over the Shropshire countryside.

If you have left your car here then it sounds like you're only doing the 6.8 linear. Which is fine, otherwise...

Completing the Circular
From the car park main entrance walk straight across the lane to a FP on the other side with an enclosed horse track on L. Follow this path which will soon join the path you came in on, so turn L when you meet it, keeping the horse track on your L, all the way to the junction with the concrete lane. Turn L here (you came in earlier on the same track from your right).

On reaching a crossroads of tracks turn R through a gate to walk slightly uphill with hedge on both sides. As you descend, pass dog kennels on R to reach a road. Turn R and just past a turning on R signed TNC, climb the gate on L, just before the road ramp
⑦.
There is no FP sign but it is a public right of way. Keep fairly close to the fence, and then hedge, on R as you walk across this field. As you reach the top of a rise head for the remains of a metal gate ahead, but on the other side of a ditch. Cross

over the ditch as best you can and climb over the gate, being careful to avoid the barbed wire. Turn right in a small scrubby area to a wooden fence. Climb it and turn L keeping the hedge on L all the way to a gate leading to a lane.

At the time of writing this lane is undergoing a possible change to bridleway from private road so I'm rather hoping this has taken place by the time you read this. On reaching this road turn R to walk slightly uphill and past the Crematorium. The road swings L and then R and ends at the busy A5. Using the central reservation cross carefully over to the lane straight in front.

Follow this long but quiet road until eventually – after about 30 mins – pass under the M54 and turn L along the road ⑧. Take care here with traffic as there are no verges for part of the way. In around 15 mins turn R onto Haughton Lane (although there's nothing to indicate that this is Haughton Lane until you reach the other end). This long lane deposits you at a traffic island. Turn L here and walk back to the centre of Shifnal. Well done if you did all 11.7 miles!

Walk 15. Weston Park - linear

Distance: 6.4 miles

Time to allow: 3½ hrs without stops

Refreshments: Café and restaurant at Weston Park. Or take a picnic and rest in the parkland (Check opening times).

Return transport: Requires 2 cars or taxi. At the time of writing there is no direct bus route but it may be worth checking..

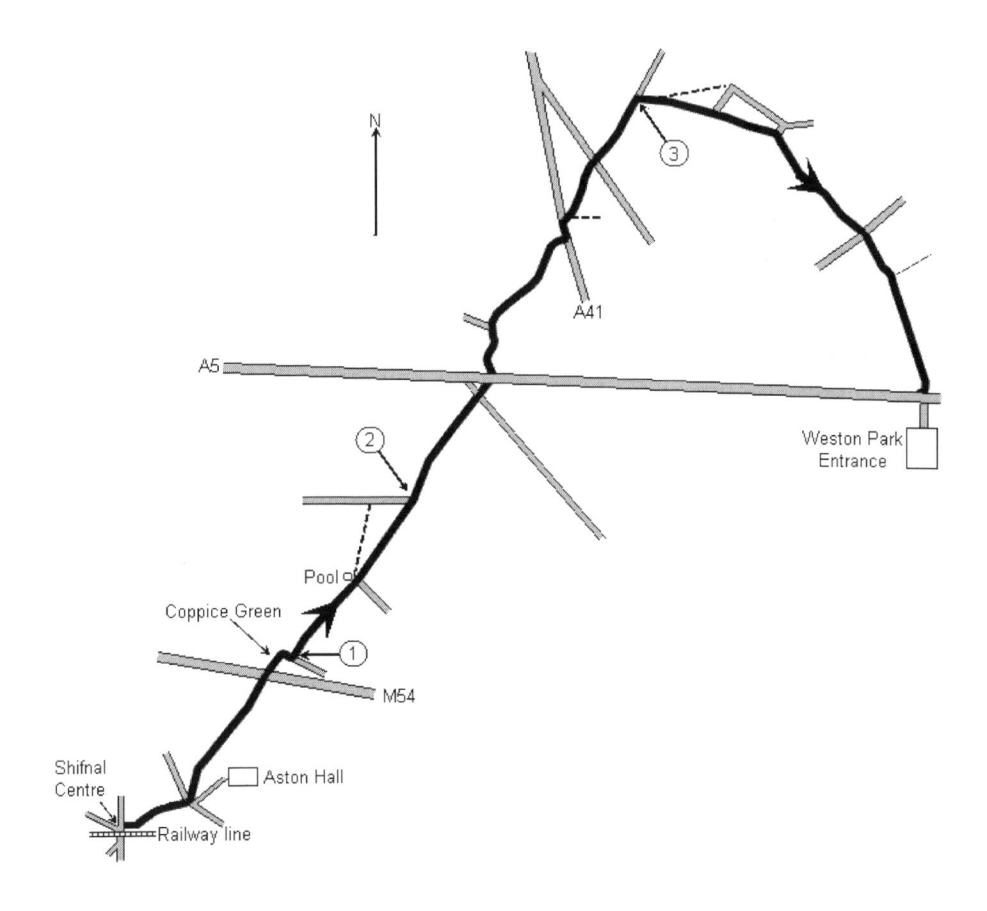

87

A very pleasant walk mainly along quiet country lanes with just one short stretch across an easy field path. The route avoids walking along any busy roads (bar a few very short yards on a wide grassy verge at the A41) and culminates by simply crossing the A5 to the entrance of Weston Park with all its amenities.

You can simply partake of refreshment in the splendid café and deli or with a prior booking a full meal at The Granary restaurant.

There is a small charge to enter the extensive 1000 acre parkland where you can explore the huge deer park, the colourful and enchanting formal gardens, the magnificent 17th century stately home, adventure playground in the woods, the train around the lake and so much more. Remember to check opening times prior to your walk.

Start the walk from the centre of Shifnal at the Millennium Clock. With your back to Katrina's Card Shop, cross the road and head along Aston Street with railway tunnels to your R. Pass the Railway Inn and further on The Village Hall to your L.

Keep along Aston Street to reach crossroads. Walk straight over and head up Coppice Green Lane past Idsall School on L. Eventually cross the M54 to Coppice Green. Follow the lane as it turns sharp R and in a few yards take FP on L just beyond a tree ① and follow this FP through 3 fields going uphill and then down to a fishing pool at the bottom.

Before descending turn and look around; on the skyline to your left is the prominent Titterstone Clee Hill and nearby Shropshire's highest - Brown Clee Hill at 540m – 1772'. Moving round you will see the tall chimney of Ironbridge Power Station.

On reaching the lane at the pool and corner turn L to walk along the length of this delightfully peaceful tree-lined avenue to eventually reach a junction with another lane. Turn R past the entrance to Lizard Wood following the lane as it bends L.

②

Ignoring the FP at the side of the wood continue along the lane. As an alternative there is a Permissive Path which runs alongside the lane. Choose between grassy path and tarmac road – they meet further on.

When you reach lane crossroads continue straight on and in a few yards carefully cross the A5 onto another quiet lane to Burlington. A few minutes after crossing the ford by the footbridge, ignore a L lane and continue in the same direction, eventually reaching the A41. Turn L and in a few yards turn R along another lane.

Cross over another road and shortly after passing Crossroads Farm on L take the lane on R with a sign marked Blymhill and Weston-under-Lizard and a separate finger post marked Blymhill Common.

③

Keep on this fairly long lane ignoring other lanes off L. On reaching crossroads with Hatch Lane go straightover to walk along Beighterton Lane.

The lane ends some time later at the noisy A5 once more. Carefully cross to the entrance to Weston Park. Walk straight down the road to the reception at The Granary where refreshments are available.

Walk 16. The Shrewsbury Arms at Albrighton – linear

Distance: 6.8 miles
Time to allow: 3½ hrs without stops
Refreshments: Café David Austin Roses.
　　　　　　　Shrewsbury Arms end of walk.
　　　　　　　Tea rooms in Albrighton
Return Transport. Bus stop next to
　　　　　　　Shrewsbury Arms.
　　　　　　　Train station ¾ mile.
　　　　　　　Taxi firm on Station Road.

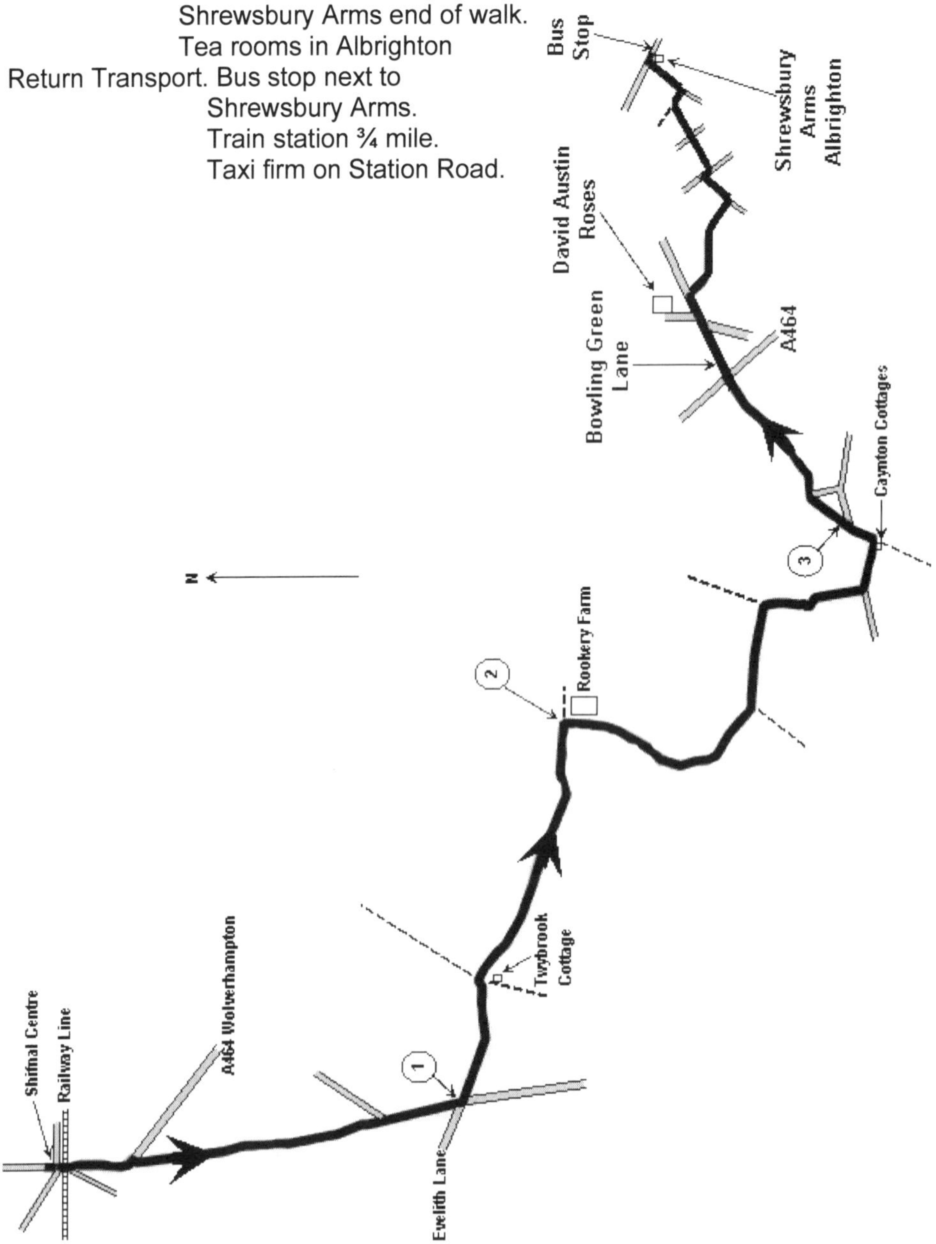

This lovely walk visits Shifnal's nearest easterly town along quiet lanes, field paths and through woodland meeting up with the River Worfe for a few brief moments, before ending in Albrighton at the superb 17th century Shrewsbury Arms.

Start the walk from the centre of Shifnal at the Millennium Clock and head south under the railway bridge, passing the Odfellows pub and the Park House Hotel. As the road bends to the left turn right up **Park Lane** (signed Ryton & Grindleforge), past St Andrews School and walk alongside a superb row of mature trees of oak, sycamore, holly, horse chestnut and beech.

Soon the houses disappear as the lane narrows and becomes much quieter. Pass between sandstone walls and continue down this delightful straight and narrow lane for about 10 minutes (1/3 of a mile). This is Hinnington Road. Turn L on the bridleway ① opposite the turn for Evelith Lane.

This is part of the 615 mile long-distance path The Monarch's Way which traces the route taken by Charles II after his defeat at the Battle of Worcester in 1651.

You will soon come to a gate. Follow the FP signs and walk alongside the grounds of a large house. As you travel this wide grassy ride you will see Twybrook Cottage ahead. The path goes through a small copse. Turn L when you reach Twybrook Cottage and then almost immediately turn R on FP which runs alongside the grounds of the cottage, with a small stream seen through the trees on your R.

Watch out for startled pheasants which may in fact startle you too!

As the trees end you will see a tall, white marker post – continue straight on across this field rising slightly and you will soon see another tall, white marker post. Aim for this and then go through the trees, down a farm track which runs out to a metalled lane with a charmingly remote cottage on your R.

Carry straight on along this lane as it rises slightly. When it bends continue straight on over a stile onto a FP, passing 6 large fir trees on your L. Keep on with a small wooded area on your L. On reaching the lane turn L and walk along it, with large pools either side.

Walk past the 2 unnamed cottages on your L (marked as Birdswood Cottages on the OS map) and when you reach the farm buildings of Rookery Farm ② turn sharp R on the FP running alongside the buildings. This is a long farm track leading to trees.

As you reach a hedge the path goes across the next field to a stile and marker post and into the woods (if the field is ploughed or crops are high turn L and follow the field boundary to the stile). Here you enter the woodland and you'll soon see the River Worfe below L. This lovely little woodland path descends to a field.

<u>Keep your navigational wits about you for this little stretch as there's no clear path:</u> when you reach the field turn R and then immediately L, down towards a bend in the river (which, at this stage, looks more like a stream than a river). You'll see another tall, white marker post near the bridge crossing the river.

Follow the path as it bends R and then L uphill to farm buildings high up on the right – look out for a waymarker on a tree as a confirmer. On reaching the top, continue straight on along the track, keeping all farm buildings on your R and a few yards on, go through a gate with a waymarker. Here take the

BW ahead L (not the more obvious footpath R!) to walk straight on with hedge on your R.

You might just catch a glimpse of the large silver-looking building through the trees to your L – this is the Cold War Museum at RAF Cosford. Don't be surprised to hear and see quite a lot of sky activity as light planes are based here along with the Air Ambulance helicopters.

At the end of the field go through the gate and continue in the same direction, again keeping hedge on your R (the path may be overgrown in summer but still navigable). On reaching a junction with a farm track, turn R along it towards Atchley House.

Follow the track as it swings L of the house with a holly hedge on your R, all the way to a road. Turn L and walk along it past Caynton Cottages at a sharp L bend.

Just after that, as the road bends to the R, follow the FP on L ③ (sign hidden behind telegraph pole) that heads diagonally across, to join another lane at another sharp bend. You're now back on The Monarch's Way again and at the time of writing a BW has been created on your L which takes you off the lane to run alongside it.

Continue to the often busy A464. Cross carefully and continue in the same direction along Bowling Green Lane. Once again a BW runs alongside for part of the way which is better than walking along the lane.

The BW ends just before aircraft hangars at RAF Cosford's perimeter fence and a narrow path drops you down to continue along Bowling Green Lane.

In a few yards there is an optional visit to David Austin Roses down a lane off L – Old Worcester Road – it will take you about 5 minutes off route, (look out for the brown leisure sign) with café, toilets and an opportunity to stock your garden with new plants, the only restricting factor being the amount of empty space in your rucksack!

In about 175 yards from the David Austin Roses sign, take the FP on R at a metal double gate. You will see a windmill (now a residential home complete with room atop making it look like a watchtower) across the fields ahead left which marks the end of this short FP.

If the path is not obvious, (depending on field crop) head in the general direction of the windmill towards a tree where you'll meet a marker post. This will guide you to a stile just to the left of a white house.

Climb the stile and follow the path which leads to a drive. Continue in same direction, past the windmill now on your R, to a road.

Turn L to walk along the road and on reaching a road junction turn R and then almost immediately, turn L to walk through houses along Talbot Road. At crossroads carry straight on in the same direction.

When you arrive at the end of the cul-de-sac take a path off R between houses and shortly turn L upon reaching another road which will bring you rather neatly to The Shrewsbury Arms* with the church** opposite and the Shifnal bus stop just past the pub on the same side. Enjoy the drink!

*This lovely old 3-storey building (The Shrewsbury Arms) is thought to have originally been built as a manor house in the 17th century and is now a Grade II Listed Building.

**The 12th Century church of St Mary Magdalene which boasts a ring of 8 bells, is the resting place of a number of Earls of Shrewsbury and the only Duke of Shrewsbury 1660 - 1718. There are also tea rooms on Station Road which is where you'll be heading to catch your train if that's your preferred mode of transport for your return to Shifnal – the station is about ¾ of a mile away and will take around 20 minutes from the pub. The tea rooms are less than 10 minutes away.

To reach either or both; on arrival at the road junction at The Shrewsbury Arms turn R to walk along the High Street and just past The Old Bush and before The Crown pub, turn L at crossroads to walk down Station Road where you'll have a choice of two tea rooms on the left.***

There is also a taxi firm here if you prefer that to the extra walk down to the station which will take you a further 10 minutes or so. You'll need Platform 2.

***You will have just passed the Millennium Clock made by J. B. Joyce & Co, founded in Shropshire and who claim to be the oldest clock manufacturer in the world, originally established in 1690. You might spot the similarity to the one in Shifnal at the start of the walk– it's the same manufacturer!

Walk 17. ✧ Granville Nature Reserve – linear or circular – you choose! *See Walk 14 for map and instructions*

Linear: Distance: 6.8
Time to allow: 3¾ hrs without stops
Transport: 2 cars, taxi or bus from Asda for return
Refreshments: Suggest picnic lunch on arrival at the reserve.
Circular: Distance: 11.7 miles
Time to allow: 6 hrs without stops
Refreshments: Suggest picnic lunch on arrival at the reserve. Pubs and tea rooms in Shifnal

This is an excellent 6.8 miles route from Shifnal to Granville Nature Reserve taking in the source of Wesley Brook at The Flash. Not too long after you will reach delightful Granville Nature Reserve which is just such a lovely setting for a picnic – wonderful views from the 'The Top of the World' and surrounded by nature at its best.

There are then three distinct alternatives for returning to Shifnal:-

4) <u>Car.</u> *With 2 cars available leave a car at the reserve car park to drive back*

5) <u>Bus.</u> *Exit the Granville Nature Reserve car park at the main gate and turn R to walk along the lane for about 20 minutes to the roundabout, cross over and pick up a bus to Telford at the Asda store. From here another bus will take you back to Shifnal (check timetables beforehand).*

6) <u>Walk.</u> *Turn this linear walk into a circular – you're over half way at this point – it's just 4.9 miles (about 2½ hrs) back to Shifnal.*

NB: This walk has been given the ✧ symbol as there are a couple of unavoidable but short sections through housing estates and a trading estate but the few minutes spent should not detract from an otherwise splendid walk.

Walk 18. Ironbridge - linear

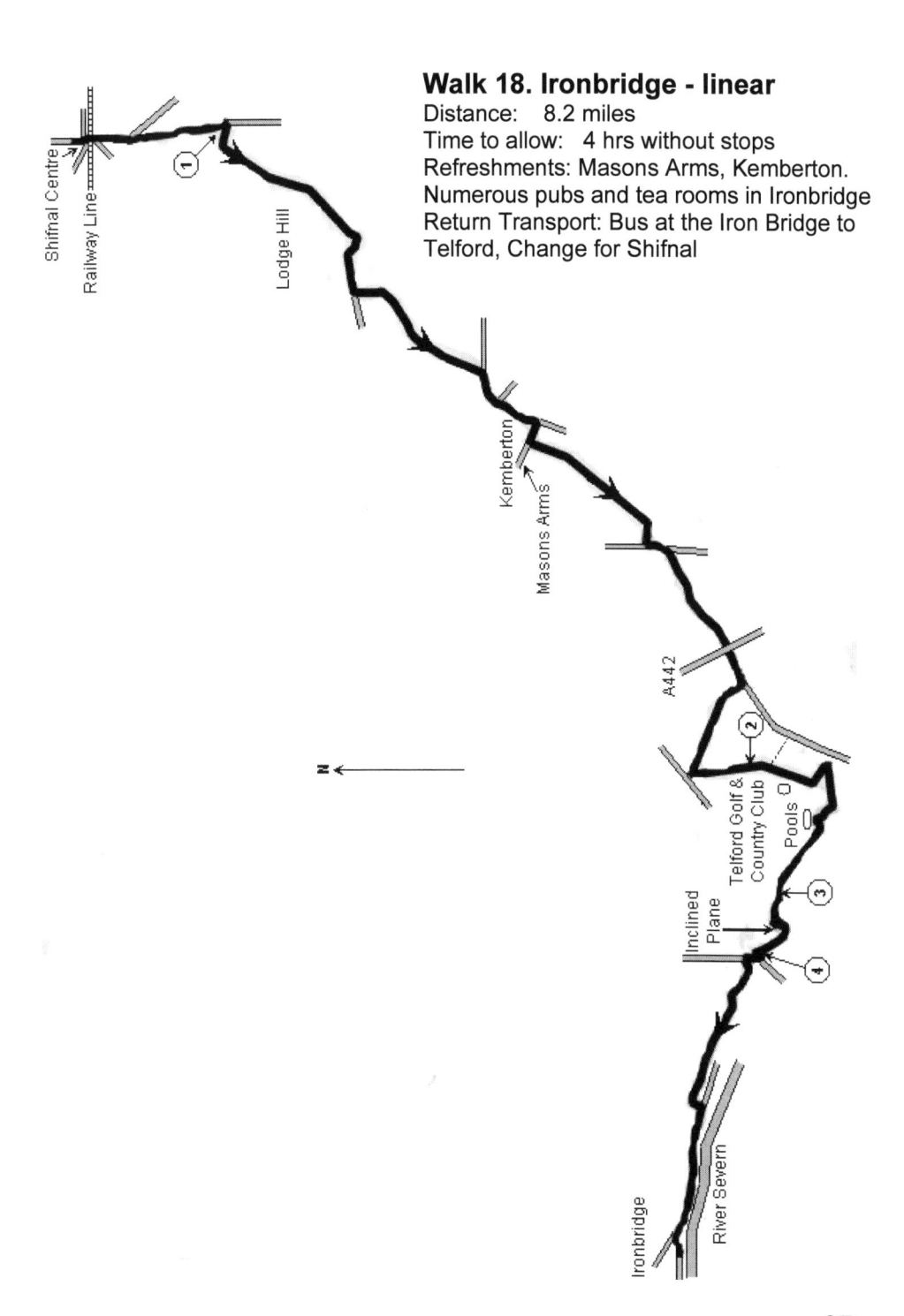

Distance: 8.2 miles
Time to allow: 4 hrs without stops
Refreshments: Masons Arms, Kemberton.
Numerous pubs and tea rooms in Ironbridge
Return Transport: Bus at the Iron Bridge to Telford, Change for Shifnal

97

A splendid walk from the centre of Shifnal to the busy and lively centre at Ironbridge culminating at the famous bridge itself. The route follows footpaths, bridleways, quiet lanes and a golf course, taking in superb woodland, fields and views on its way. One not to miss!

Start the walk from the centre of Shifnal at the Millennium Clock and head south under the railway bridge, passing the Odfellows pub and the Park House Hotel. As the road bends L turn R up Park Lane (signed Ryton & Grindleforge), past St Andrews School and walk alongside a superb row of mature trees of oak, sycamore, holly, horse chestnut and beech.

A few minutes past the turning for Lodge Hill Farm take the FP on the R ① past a bungalow, over a stile and on to a wide track with pool on L. The track soon bends sharply L and heads slightly uphill with a hedge on L and fence on R. Then as it bends slightly left it changes to hedge now on R and fence on L. Go through a gate or climb the stile to walk with fence on R (you will see The Wrekin in the distance, in front and to your R) to the top of Lodge Hill.

You will have hardly noticed the climb but in a short while you'll be at the top with a wonderful vista for your eyes to feast upon.

Ahead you'll see Shropshire's highest hill, Brown Clee complete with masts and to its left Titterstone Clee (Shropshire's third highest hill) which has an Earth Satellite in the shape of a golf ball near its summit. On a clear day you can see The Malvern Hills ahead and to the left. Looking straight ahead you will see a tall chimney – this is Ironbridge Power Station with its cooling towers just out of sight sitting in Ironbridge Gorge and our destination. Benthall Edge is also visible behind and to the L of the chimney.

Continue in the same direction downhill keeping the fence on R to a stile where you enter woods soon to pass a bench. Follow the path down George's Steps and eventually reach a footbridge over Wesley Brook.

Cross the brook and turn R up this sometimes muddy path and when it meets a lane turn L to walk along it. In about 5 or 6 minutes turn L along another lane (signed 'Unsuitable for HGV's') and follow this quiet hedge-lined lane for about ten minutes. This is Field Lane but you don't know that until you reach the end of it when it reaches the junction with Mill Lane. Here turn R into Kemberton village.

As Mill Lane swings L look out for the tiny Kaleidoscope Theatre set in the grounds of Kemberton Hall. The theatre was set up to help Downs Syndrome children develop communication and drama skills.

Follow the road through Kemberton and not long after passing the church on your R turn up the lane on your R. As you reach the top you will see The Wrekin once more straight ahead and before you get to the pub – The Masons Arms – turn L along a wide FP which is actually a track to a farm. You will see the Ironbridge Power Station chimney again with the Ironbridge Gorge running to the left of it.

(At this point and if your timing is right you may, of course, wish to partake of refreshment at the excellent Masons Arms!)

When the hedge on your L ends look right for a FP waymark sign and walk diagonally across this field passing a line of 4 trees on your L to a kissing gate in the fence on the other side. (This path may not be obvious especially if the field is in crop).

Keep on in the same direction to another kissing gate by a small oak tree. This is actually a pair of kissing gates across a ditch. Continue in the same direction heading for the long farm building ahead. There's often electric fencing here so cross with care to a small gate in the fence, cross over a farm track and shortly walk with the long farm building and bank to your L arriving at a kissing gate to a road in a few yards.

Turn L and walk along the road for a few yards and then take the next R and walk along the lane into Brockton, passing the rather impressive Brockton House set in fine grounds.

Walk through this charming little village until you arrive at the busy A442 road to Bridgnorth. Carefully cross straightover to walk uphill on the road opposite and in a couple of minutes turn R along Brick Kiln Lane past a row houses on your R.

When almost at the end of the row look out for a waymarker on the L and head across to a stile (often overgrown) on the other side of this field. Keeping in the same direction, head just to the R of the tree you see in the hedge ahead and climb the stile. Carry on in the same direction diagonally across to the corner of the field and a gate to a road.

On reaching the road turn immediate L along a track, ignoring a warning sign on the gate appertaining to access – this refers to vehicles, it is a Right of Way. When you reach the normally open gate leading into the farmyard don't go through the gate but look to your R ② and you'll see a footpath going behind a concrete fence and metal girder. It's a bit tight as it's close to the hedge and can get a little overgrown in summer but after two stiles you'll reach the Telford Golf and Country Club and be deposited unceremoniously onto the golf course. (If this very short section is too overgrown to cross, you'll find a gap in the hedge to your R which drops you onto the golf course earlier).

There used to be a path here that went straight across the fairway to Haywood but it has been modified to go around the perimeter of the golf course.

So once on the Golf Course turn L at sign – 'Warning golf balls, stay to footpath' - to walk with hedge on L and in a few yards go down a path through trees taking the L fork as you enter.

Out of the trees continue with hedge on L, soon passing a pool a few yards away on the right. When you reach a FP off L (which just leads you to the road) ignore it and continue down, still with hedge on L, (at the time of writing there is a sign here stating 'No Walking' but ignore that too!).

In a few minutes reach a perimeter fence in front of you and a wide FP – turn R here to walk with perimeter fence on L. In a few yards when you meet a wooden gate and open fence continue about 10 yards and then leave the path (which would deposit you onto a green) for a smaller FP near a tree off L to now walk very close to the perimeter fence on L. This path can be overgrown in summer but is passable.

After a few minutes the path drops down to a metal bridge over a tiny stream and then to climb steps on the other side to arrive at a pool. Turn L to walk alongside the pool on your right and just past it take a path off L into the woods away from the golf course. On reaching a path junction turn L into Haywood.

During the summer this narrow path is often overgrown but nonetheless easy to follow.

③ Depending on the time of year and if any maintenance has been carried out it's possible to make a mistake on the next section (the following 3 paragraphs) so a little extra concentration is required:

After around 7-10 minutes take the path forking L between 2 trees which are about 7' apart.

Then, in another 2 minutes, ignore a path and wooden kissing gate on L and continue in the same direction passing another marker as the path undulates and then finally drops to end at a wooden kissing gate leading into a meadow.

Follow a path slightly downhill to the R, between trees, and then aim for another waymarker ahead. The path then goes slightly uphill towards a tall chimney (in summer tree foliage may obscure this).

The chimney sits at the top of Coalport's 'Hay Inclined Plane' depicting the industrial heritage of the area. It was used to move limestone and iron ore from Blists Hill down to the River Severn for onward transportation.

You'll then reach a path junction where you'll turn L downhill (marked Coalport). The path descends, with glimpses of the inclined plane on your R, firstly on railway sleepers and then fine wooden steps to a wide track at the bottom. Turn R here to walk underneath the inclined plane. You are still on The Monarchs Way.

Pass by a viewing platform on the L and in around 5 minutes look out for a path with FP sign which turns sharp L downhill ④. In a few yards the path forks. Take the right fork to the sometimes busy road below. Care is needed here as the path drops straight on to the road. Cross carefully turning R uphill and just past the house (The Grooms House) turn L along a Permissive Path, through a gate and skirting a wood.

This ancient woodland is Lloyds Coppice. As you head deeper into it, turn L at a path junction.

In a few yards look to the right and you'll see the remains of an icehouse which used to supply the fine Madeley Wood Hall which is just about all that remains of this once grand estate. Follow the signs for Ironbridge and you'll eventually reach the main road into Ironbridge at a point where Wesley Road also joins it. Turn R here (NOT along Wesley Road) and walk along the main road beside the River Severn for about ½ mile.

As an alternative to the road, as you approach Ironbridge, some distance past Bedlam Furnaces, and just after a row of terraced houses on your left called Valentino Row, you'll see a path down to the river (marked Severnside) which you can follow right to (and under) the Iron Bridge itself and into the centre of Ironbridge the town, with some interesting individual shops, along with a plethora of pubs and tea rooms. And of course – the excellent museums.

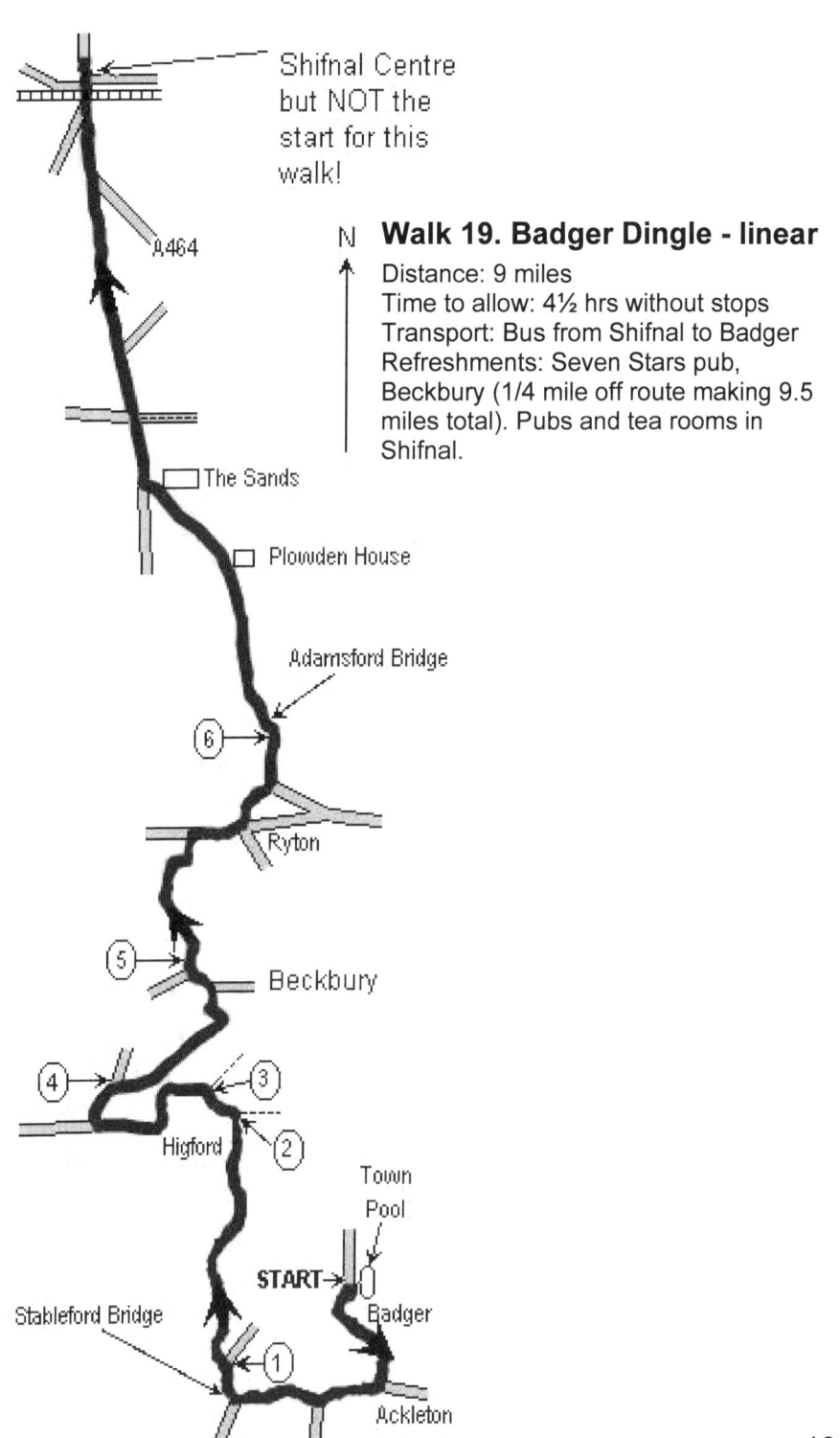

Walk 19. Badger Dingle - linear

Distance: 9 miles
Time to allow: 4½ hrs without stops
Transport: Bus from Shifnal to Badger
Refreshments: Seven Stars pub, Beckbury (1/4 mile off route making 9.5 miles total). Pubs and tea rooms in Shifnal.

104

Oh… what a delight this walk is. Another of my favourites! Badger Dingle is a splendid place to explore with sandstone rocks amidst fine woodland and a lovely stream running through which soon disgorges into the River Worfe. In fact the river features a few times during this superb walk.

The best way to tackle this walk is to catch the 114 or 113 bus from Jaspers pub, Victoria Road, Shifnal to Badger and walk back to Shifnal. This Telford to Bridgnorth bus passes through delightful villages south of Shifnal including Kemberton, Ryton and Beckbury before arriving at the tranquil village of Badger and the start of this superb walk alongside Town Pool.

Position yourself so that the pool is on your L and continue down the road in the direction of the bus you've just alighted. As the road swings to the right about 25 yards further on you will see a FP on the L. Head downhill here to the stream. At a path junction turn L and then fork R to the stream and a weir created as water escapes from a large pool on your L. In fact the stream is fed by a series of pools and ponds before arriving at the River Worfe at Stableford.

The path crosses over the stream and rises steeply uphill to exit the woods at a kissing gate, then across a field to a farm track and eventually the road at Ackleton. Turn R here and walk along the path in front of a row of houses where you'll soon be deposited onto the road. Walk along the road for about 5 minutes.

In the distance to the right, you will see The Wrekin and the chimney of Ironbridge Power Station. Looking ahead you'll also catch a glimpse of Titterstone Clee Hill – the 3rd highest hill in Shropshire. (The highest being Brown Clee followed by Stiperstones)

Soon take the FP on the R which hugs a fence to your L and soon arrives at a stile. The path continues downhill through gorse bushes to cross the river at a footbridge. Keeping the hedge to your L you'll soon arrive at a lane where turn R over Stableford Bridge. Walk along the lane and just past the Tudor-style Stableford Lodge, turn L to walk along a wide BW ① on the edge of a wood. After a short distance go through the waymarked gate on your L into an open field.

Go straight ahead keeping trees and a slope into marshy ground on your L. Eventually, you'll arrive at a metal gate in the fence ahead. Keep in the same direction along a faint track for a short distance. It then turns slowly to the right, circling the higher ground to your R. You will soon see a gate at the side of a row of conifers. Go through the gate and turn left onto the wide track through woodland with a pool soon coming into view on L and shortly after the River Worfe.

As you leave this fine wooded area go through the gate and continue along the track as it swings R to walk between banks of gorse and scrub. Continue slightly uphill on the same wide track. Turn L and then immediate R and in a short distance turn L to descend into a delightful tree-lined gully. Follow the well-worn path through woodland once more until you come to a fork in the paths ②. Take the L path to walk with stream on your L.

At a path junction turn L again ③. The River Worfe will now be on your R. The path eventually emerges at garages onto a drive which crosses the river with houses on both sides. This is the wonderfully isolated hamlet of Higford. Go through the gate and head straight uphill along the lane.

The lane continues to rise and then descends past the impressive-looking Higford Hall School on R. At the bottom turn R at lane junction and in approximately 300 yards turn R along a BW signed Monarch's Way ④.

Continue along this well-defined path as it soon leaves woodland with a fence on your L. The path soon drops down slightly and eventually arrives at Beckbury Sewage Works.

(If in need of refreshment at this stage the rather quaint Seven Stars pub at Beckbury is a R turn along the lane for ¼ of a mile).

Turn L when reaching the road to walk uphill and take the FP on your R just past a pair of houses. Descend to a footbridge with wooded hillside beyond ⑤. Once over the footbridge climb the bank with fence on L as it rises steeply. At the top turn R keeping fence on L to a stile. Cross this and continue in the same direction but with fence now on your R.

When the fence gives in to a hedge look for a stile. Keep in the same direction again with the hedge now on your left. The corner you see ahead can be cut slightly by skirting the head of this charming little valley as it swings R. You will soon reach a gate on your L. Pass through this and walk along the straight farm track to the lane where you turn R into Ryton.

As you cross the bridge take the next lane on the L uphill by Ryton Court and Mead Cottage to reach the church at the top. Continue along the lane past houses with grand names such as Ryton Grange, Ryton Hall and Ryton Heights and just past the white building on the L - Church Farm House - take the FP at the side and walk with hedge on L to a gate. Go through and descend a lovely sunken wooded pathway.

As you emerge to flatter ground turn L in a few yards ⑥ over Adamsford Bridge (unmarked) to follow a wide farm track for about a mile, passing the isolated Plowden House on the way and finally reaching Hinnington Road past houses known as The Sands.

Turn R here and follow this long, straight, narrow lane as it widens and eventually reaches houses and some time after, the main Wolverhampton road where you turn L and walk back into Shifnal.

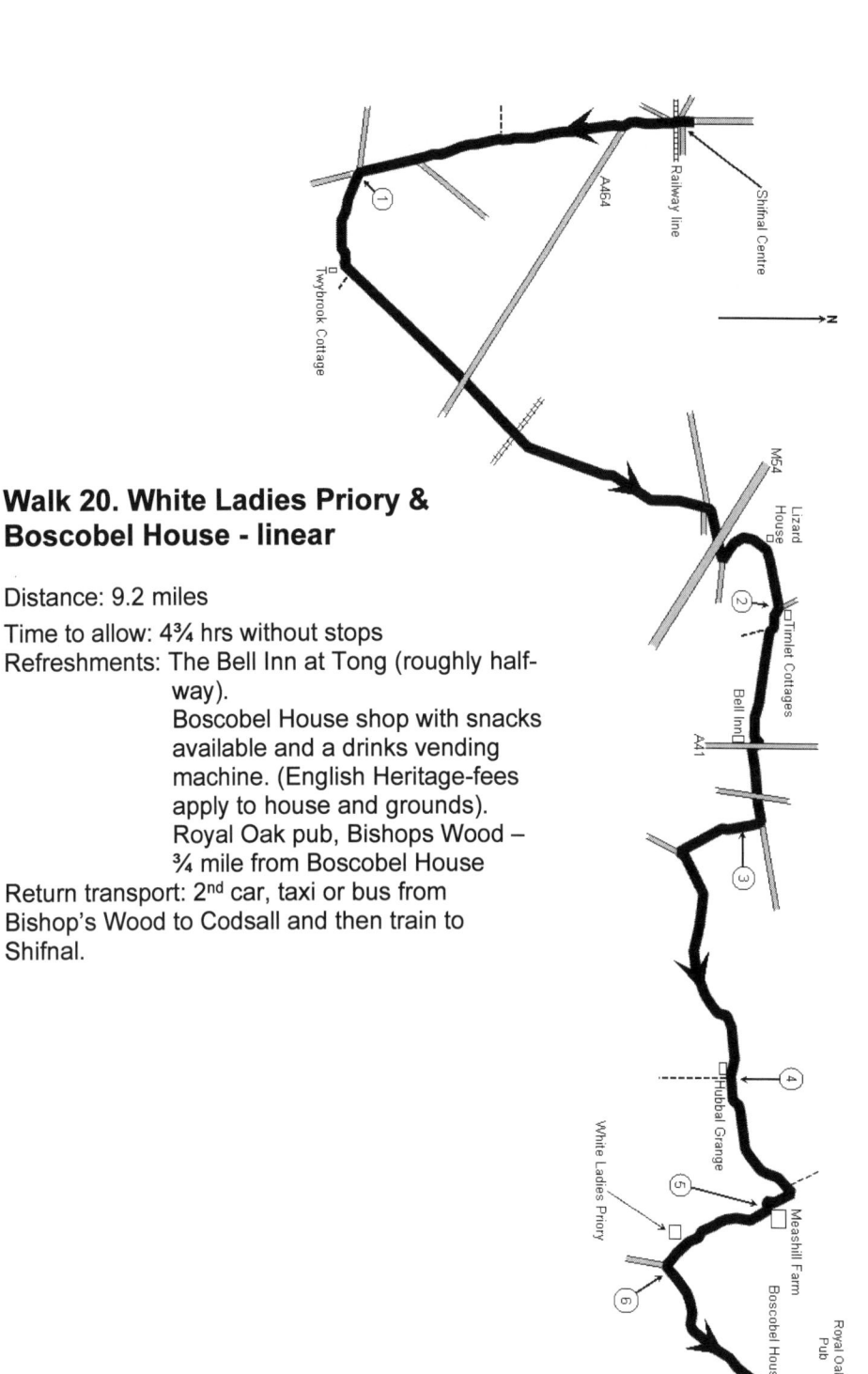

Walk 20. White Ladies Priory & Boscobel House - linear

Distance: 9.2 miles

Time to allow: 4¾ hrs without stops

Refreshments: The Bell Inn at Tong (roughly half-way).
Boscobel House shop with snacks available and a drinks vending machine. (English Heritage-fees apply to house and grounds).
Royal Oak pub, Bishops Wood – ¾ mile from Boscobel House

Return transport: 2nd car, taxi or bus from Bishop's Wood to Codsall and then train to Shifnal.

This is a lovely and rewarding linear walk with superb views across Shropshire's glorious and vast countryside ending at English Heritage's Boscobel House with refreshments available (albeit limited) but check to ensure it's open, of course.

Allow time to look around this fascinating place where King Charles II is reputed to have hidden up a tree in what is now known as the Royal Oak, when he fled from his defeat at the Battle of Worcester. The pub name Royal Oak, now used all over the country, has its roots here at Boscobel House. Often the pub sign will depict the king in a tree, sometimes including the date of the battle 1651.

In fact when you turn off the lane south of Shifnal heading towards Twybrook Cottage you will be following in the footsteps of the king as the route uses part of the 615 mile National Trail known as The Monarchs Way which will take you all the way to Boscobel House. You will often come across waymarkers depicting this trail, so there will be confirmers all along the route.

For your return to Shifnal from Boscobel House there is a bus stop at nearby Bishops Wood (¾ mile away (less than 30 mins walk)) which will take you to Codsall for a train back to Shifnal. Otherwise a 2nd car or taxi is required for the return. There is also a pub – the aptly named Royal Oak – at Bishops Wood, the bus stop being nearby. This pub was the first to be so named after the nearby oak tree at Boscobel House.

Start the walk from the centre of Shifnal at the Millennium Clock and head south under the railway bridge, passing the Odfellows pub and the Park House Hotel. As the road bends L turn R up Park Lane (signed Ryton & Grindleforge), past St Andrews School, and walk alongside a superb row of mature trees of oak, sycamore, holly, horse chestnut and beech. Soon the houses disappear as the lane narrows and becomes much quieter. Continue slightly down hill on this straight-as-a-die road until you reach a lane coming off on the R which is Evelith Lane, but <u>don't</u> turn up it.

① Turn L here along the drive with hedge on R to eventually reach the gate of a house.

This is where you pick up The Monarchs Way following it all the way to Boscobel House. Try to imagine the king travelling along here as quickly as he could to escape Cromwell's men who were in hot pursuit!

Arriving at the gate a FP goes to the R and then L as it skirts the house, through a small wooded area and eventually reaches Twybrook Cottage. Turn L here along this wide and peaceful track for 2 miles, crossing the A464 and some time after, the Birmingham-Shrewsbury railway line at Bonemill Bridge. Keep following the main drive past 2 houses on R. Just past the second house there's a gate which may be closed displaying a 'Private Drive' sign, ignore the sign and go through the gate – this is a public right of way, and confirmed by a Monarch's Way marker on the right-hand post.

Continue on this wide drive with hedge on R and in a few yards enter a wooded area, eventually arriving at another main road near **Neachley Lane**.

Cross this often fast and busy road and walk R to pass under the M54. Just after turn L along a much quieter road past

Lizard House and some time later, when you reach a sharp left at Timlet Cottages, turn R down a wide BW between 2 white posts. ②

Pass a house with pool on L and another pool through the hedge on R. When you reach another house with a drive turn L to walk uphill parallel to the drive and into a field. Keep walking in the same direction, keeping the hedge on R, until you reach the main A41 road.

Cross carefully to the R and go down the lane opposite the Bell Inn. *(If the timing's right you could, of course, pop in to this fine old inn for halfway refreshments).*

Walk down the lane – to Tong Norton. On reaching crossroads continue straight over (signed Bishops Wood & Brewood) and in a few yards turn R to walk along Shaw Lane. When the lane ends in front of the last house on L, the route continues as a FP in the same direction. ③

As you walk through the fields keeping hedge on L you'll see Tong Church ahead. After a series of stiles (and electric fences at the time of writing) a lane is reached. Turn L to follow the lane shortly passing Tong Hill Farm. The lane which starts as a surfaced road soon turns into a soft wide bridleway track known as Hubbal Lane, it will become obvious why in a few minutes.

According to an information sign (which was sited here some months ago but more recently has mysteriously disappeared) a wide variety of wildlife is to be seen along this delightful path including (depending on season) lapwing, linnets, swallows, tree sparrows, kestrels, house martins, buzzard, skylark and brown hare. Add to this 2 dead moles that I came across on 2 separate occasions. What happens to moles here?! Perhaps they pop up to witness the rich and varied wildlife and then succumb to it!

Wildflowers to be spotted through the year include, Red Campion, Greater Stitchwort, Bluebells, Buttercups, Yellow Archangel, Common Vetch, Herb Robert and further on in the field edges; Creeping Cinquefoil and the exquisite Scarlet Pimpernel.

On a warm sunny day you might also spot a few species of moth. I've seen Burnet moths, Silver Y, Nettle-tap and Silver-ground Carpet along with butterflies such as Meadow Brown, Large and Small Skippers, Ringlet, Peacock, Small Tortoiseshell, Comma, Red Admiral, Speckled Wood and many others all enjoying this wildlife haven. You might also be lucky enough to see a Dragonfly – most probably a Brown Hawker. If you keep your eyes peeled on a warm summer's day you'll certainly see Common Blue Damselflies.

Keep straight on for about 20-30 mins, ignoring any paths off L or R and eventually you'll arrive at a finger post at Hubbal Grange – a building which is no more, but nonetheless, an area of great historical importance.

④

An inscription on the post gives this information.

'Site of Hobbal* Grange behind you. Birthplace of the Penderel* Brothers. On 4-9-1651 King Charles II rested here after his defeat at the Battle of Worcester on the 3-9-1651. Presented by The Pendrill* Family History Society to commemorate the restoration of the monarchy May 29 1660-2010'.

As I write in 2013 I'm more than happy to report that the monarchy still exists!

(*There appears to be at least 3 ways of spelling Penderel, 2 of which appear in the few lines on the plaque! Also, and more curiously, the wording on the plaque has incorrectly named the house Hobbal Grange instead of Hubbal!)

You might want to turn R for a few yards and use your imagination in an attempt to 'see' Hubbal Grange as it would have been but return to the finger post afterwards to continue along the main path.

Pause for a few seconds to imagine the scene as you glimpse, through the trees, the site of what would have been a quite splendid-looking house. In fact a fair bit of imagination is required here as the ruins of the timber-framed building are now overgrown by nettles and brambles.

This section of the Monarch's Way shoots off the main Monarch's Way and was done in both directions by the fugitive prince as he backtracked in desperation to avoid capture.

Return to the finger post and continue on the main track. Eventually you will see a house and buildings ahead – this is Meashill Farm which you'll be passing through shortly. The path swings L and then a few minutes later meets a lane. Turn R here towards the farmhouse.

As you approach you will see the drive forks.

⑤

Take the L fork to pass in front of the house and go through a wide metal gate to walk diagonally across the stable yard and you'll see a marker on the wall where the path continues behind wooden boards. This drops you onto a path now heading away from the farm with a hedge on L.

As you emerge into a field you'll see to the right the silver-topped Cold War Museum at RAF Cosford. Beyond and just to the left is Shropshire's highest hill – Brown Clee, and to the left of that the third highest – Titterstone Clee. Shortly, coming in to view just to the right of the Cold War building, you'll see The Wrekin and between the two you should be able to spot the tall, thin chimney that is Ironbridge Power Station with the wooded hill of Benthall Edge to the side.

The path continues along the field edge, soon entering a delightfully wooded area with many more wildflowers to spot.

Soon looking R through the trees you will see the ruins of White Ladies Priory and a little further on, a gate leading into the site where you are free to wander and enjoy this tranquil spot. An information board tells us this was a 12C nunnery and was used by King Charles II to hide from the parliamentarians before seeking refuge at Boscobel House.

This is an enchanting and atmospheric place, and one that is little visited (although I suspect weekends might bring a handful of folk), maybe because it's not easy to get to and there is no car park. Although it's only a few minutes walk from Boscobel House few people take the trouble and that's a pity. Or is it? Perhaps it's best to keep this jewel a slightly hidden secret. I've been here on days with pouring rain and deep snow, times when it's been very cold but dry and many a day in the heat of summer yet rarely encountered a soul – except for the mythical and the mystical. Yes – let's keep it secret! It's a magical place.

Return to the gate and continue along the path to reach a lane. Turn L here to walk along the lane, eventually arriving at Boscobel House BUT…

⑥

Actually, there is a far better alternative to walking along the lane; in a few yards take the Permissive Path on the R which runs adjacent to the lane but affords better views with the added benefit that you don't have to climb the verge to escape the odd vehicle. This path deposits you directly at Boscobel House and you've just crossed the county border into Staffordshire!

After visiting this splendidly historic building and garden if you turn R at the main entrance and then L in a few yards this lane will take you to the Royal Oak pub in Bishops Wood (about ¾ of a mile). The bus stop is near the pub.

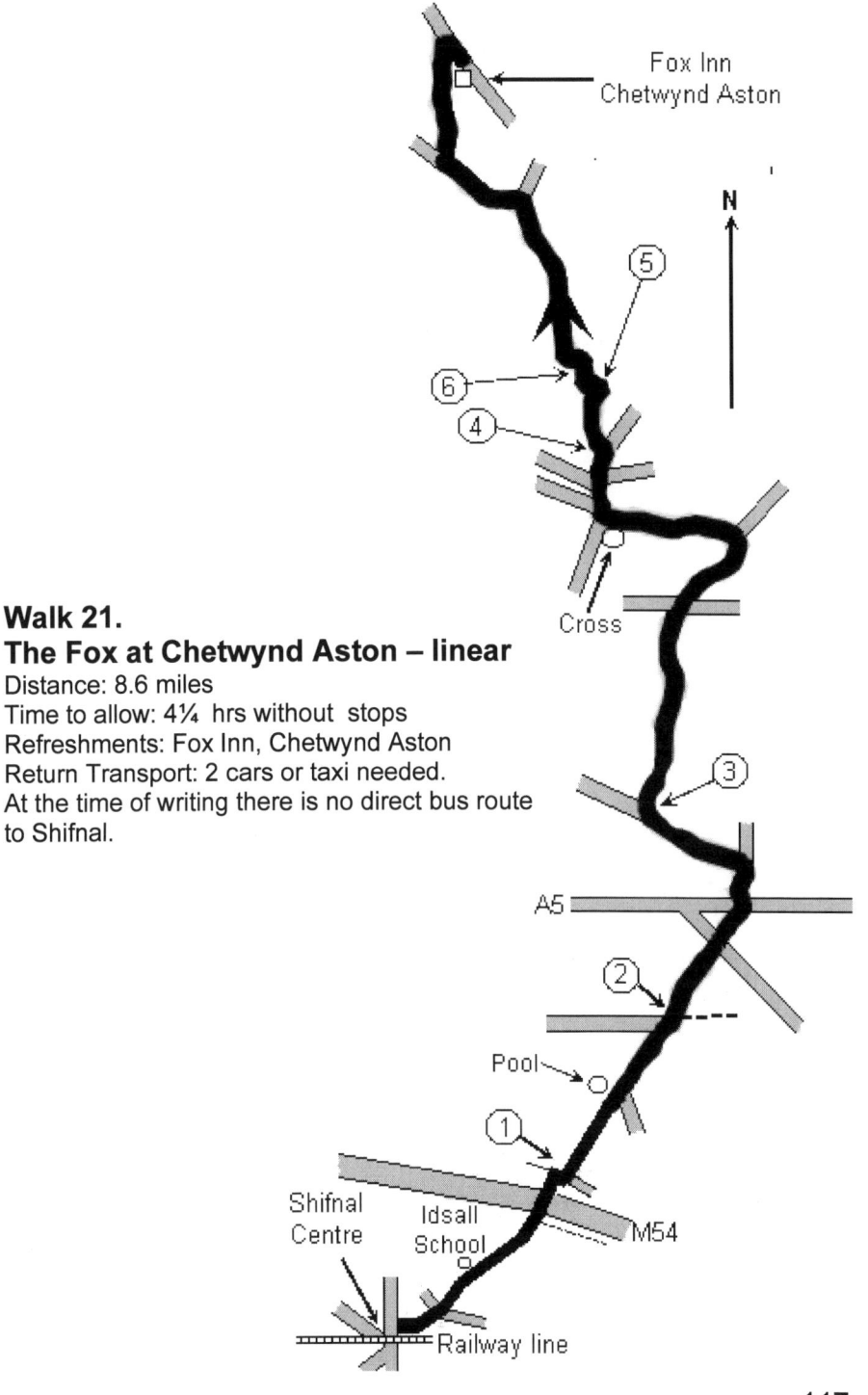

Walk 21.
The Fox at Chetwynd Aston – linear
Distance: 8.6 miles
Time to allow: 4¼ hrs without stops
Refreshments: Fox Inn, Chetwynd Aston
Return Transport: 2 cars or taxi needed.
At the time of writing there is no direct bus route to Shifnal.

117

A terrific walk through lovely countryside north of Shifnal taking in quiet lanes, woodland walks, ancient tracks and pleasant field paths ending at the award winning Edwardian-style Fox Inn at Chetwynd Aston. Time the walk to end at the pub for refreshments.

Start the walk from the centre of Shifnal at the Millennium Clock. With your back to Katrina's Card Shop cross the road and head along Aston Street with railway tunnels to your R. Pass the Railway Inn and further on The Village Hall to your L.

Keep along Aston Street to reach crossroads. Walk straight over and head up Coppice Green Lane, past Idsall School on L. Eventually cross the M54 to Coppice Green. Follow the lane as it turns sharp R and in a few yards take FP on L just beyond a tree ① and follow this FP through 3 fields, going uphill and then down to a fishing pool at the bottom. *Before descending turn and look around; on the skyline to L is the prominent Titterstone Clee Hill and nearby Shropshire's highest - Brown Clee Hill at 540m – 1772' above sea level. Moving round you will see the tall chimney of Ironbridge Power Station.*

On reaching the lane at the pool and corner turn L to walk along the length of this delightfully peaceful tree-lined avenue to eventually reach a junction with another lane. Turn R passing the entrance to Lizard Wood and follow the lane as it bends L.

②

Continue along the lane. As an alternative, in a few yards there is a Permissive Path which runs alongside the lane to its R. Choose between grassy path and tarmac road – they meet further on (if using the Permissive Path keep an eye out for the exit point back on to the road, as at the time of writing it wasn't obvious).

When you reach lane crossroads continue straight on and in a few yards carefully cross the A5 onto another quiet lane (signed Burlington). A few minutes after crossing the ford by the footbridge take the lane off L.

After about 15 mins take the bridleway on R (signposted). ③

This is a wide track that keeps in the same direction and in a short while passes through a farm yard which includes Ted's Farm Shop, Sherrifhales. *You might spot a Peacock as you walk through the farmyard, you'll certainly see hens pecking around and perhaps a piglet or two.*

On reaching a junction go straight over, through a gate into a campsite and walk this field with wood on R. Over the next stile keep straight on slightly downhill, ignoring stile on R and keeping fence on R, to then walk with another wood on R. The path runs into the edge of this lovely little wood with abundant wildflowers (depending on season of course).

The path soon deposits you into a field. Keep going in the same direction until you reach a lane (at the time of writing the path went through a small enclosure with pigs before reaching the lane). Cross straightover to walk along the lane opposite.

This is Damson Lane although there's no sign to tell you this. It passes through a few houses which is the tiny hamlet of Weston Heath.

A couple of minutes after passing the last house on the L and before reaching a house on R take the FP on the L (signposted) ④ to walk with hedge on L

Keep on this obvious path in the same general direction through fields and then a very pleasant tree-lined area (although in summer this tends to be overgrown with nettles. If so bash/tread them down well, making it easier for the next happy band of 'Walks Out of Shifnal' walkers!).

When you reach a road turn R but look to the L first where you'll see the remains of an old stone cross which I believe marks the site of a once thriving medieval market place.
So, turn R to walk down the road and through Heath Hill. Once out of the village keep on the road and you will see a large wood ahead. As you reach it take the wide-tracked BW (signed) on L just before a house and the wood.

The track follows the edge of the wood but be careful not to walk the whole length of the wood. ⑤ Look out for a post with arrow which turns you L at right-angles across a field to a small metal gate you see on the other side. The path then turns R to walk with hedge on R and then a wood on R.

⑥Take care again looking out now for 3 trees in a line ahead and turn L here – again at right-angles - to walk with these 3 trees on your R going slightly uphill. This is a wide farm track between fields which soon turns sharp R to follow hedge and woodland on L.

Continue along this wide track and when you see a gap in the hedge look left and you should be able to spot a spire coming out of the trees in the distance. *This is a memorial to the 1st Duke of Sutherland on top of Lilleshall Hill.*

This is a lovely part of the walk with many wildflowers in the hedgerows and on a warm day butterflies skip along the edges. Many birds are to be seen here too with skylark, lapwing, buzzard and yellow hammer to name but a few.

Keep on the same general direction with splendid views on both sides. Eventually, after 20-30 mins you'll reach a lane where you'll turn L to walk along it.

After 5 -10 minutes reach a crossroads of lanes. Turn R here through white wooden posts and walk along this tranquil lane enjoying the mixed songs of numerous bird species.

The lane soon reaches a very ornate wrought iron fence complete with gates (open) indicating the entrance to Lilleshall Sports Centre and deposits you onto a B road.

Turn R to walk along this sometimes busy road but it's only a few very short minutes before you reach the end of your walk at the Fox Inn, Chetwynd Aston. Have a pint for me!

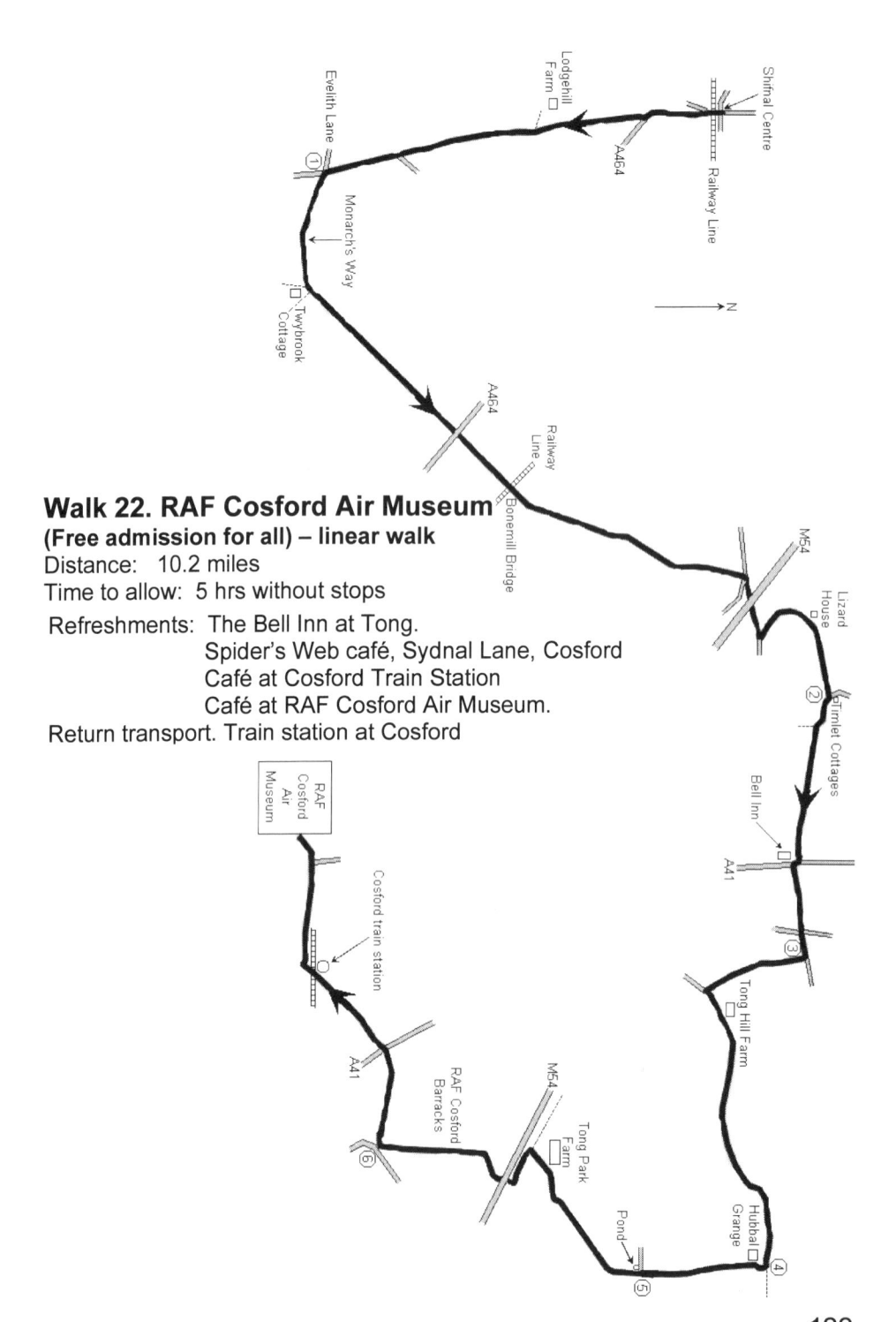

Walk 22. RAF Cosford Air Museum
(Free admission for all) – linear walk
Distance: 10.2 miles
Time to allow: 5 hrs without stops

Refreshments: The Bell Inn at Tong.
  Spider's Web café, Sydnal Lane, Cosford
  Café at Cosford Train Station
  Café at RAF Cosford Air Museum.
Return transport. Train station at Cosford

This is a lovely and rewarding linear walk following The Monarch's Way for much of the route, culminating at RAF Cosford's brilliant Air Museum which offers free admission to all and is open almost every day of the year. (Make sure you check first though!)

Allow plenty of time to look around this extraordinary homage to the planes of a by-gone age including the fascinating National Cold War Museum. Refreshments are available in the museum café and at other places en route.

There is a train station less than half-a-mile from the entrance, for your return to Shifnal.

This isn't the quickest route from Shifnal to RAF Cosford but it's certainly the best, keeping the occasional busy road to a mere encounter. The countryside you'll be walking is sheer delight!

Start the walk from the centre of Shifnal at the Millennium Clock and head south under the railway bridge, passing the Odfellows pub and the Park House Hotel. As the road bends L turn R up Park Lane (signed Ryton & Grindleforge), past St Andrews School and walk alongside a superb row of mature trees of oak, sycamore, holly, horse chestnut and beech.

Soon the houses disappear as the lane narrows and becomes much quieter. Continue slightly down hill on this straight-as-a-die road until you reach a lane coming off on the R which is Evelith Lane, but don't turn up it.

① Turn L here.

This is where you pick up The Monarchs Way, following it almost all the way to RAF Cosford.

Walk along the drive with hedge on R to the gate of a house.

A FP then goes off R skirting the house and then through a small wooded area to eventually reach Twybrook Cottage.

Turn L here along this wide and peaceful track for 2 miles crossing the A464 and some time after the Birmingham-Shrewsbury railway line at Bonemill Bridge.

Over the bridge, keep following the main drive past 2 houses on R. Just past the second house there's a gate ahead which may be closed displaying a 'Private Drive' sign. Ignore the sign (which I think must refer to motorists as it is a public right of way and confirmed by a Monarch's Way marker on the right-hand post) and go through the gate to continue on this wide drive with hedge on R.

In a few yards enter a wooded area, eventually arriving at the main road near Neachley Lane.

Cross this often fast and busy road and walk R to pass under the M54. Just after, turn L along a much quieter road, past Lizard House and some time later, when you reach a sharp left at Timlet Cottages, turn R down a wide BW between 2 white posts.

②

Pass a house with pool on L and another pool through the hedge on R. When you reach another house with a drive turn L to walk uphill parallel to the drive and into a field. Keep walking in the same direction keeping the hedge on R until you reach the main A41 road.

Cross carefully to the R and go down the lane opposite the Bell Inn. *(If the timing's right you could, of course, pop in to this fine old inn for halfway refreshments).*

Walk down the lane – to Tong Norton. On reaching crossroads continue straight over (signed Bishops Wood & Brewood) and in a few yards turn R to walk along Shaw Lane. When the lane ends in front of the last house on L, the route continues as a FP in the same direction. ③

As you walk through the fields keeping hedge on L you'll see Tong Church ahead. After a series of stiles (and electric fences at the time of writing) a lane is reached. Turn L to follow the lane, shortly passing Tong Hill Farm. The lane which starts as a surfaced road soon turns into a soft, wide bridleway track known as Hubbal Lane. It will become obvious why in a few minutes.

According to an information sign, which was sited here some months ago but more recently has mysteriously disappeared, a wide variety of wildlife is to be seen along this delightful path including (depending on season) lapwing, linnets, swallows, tree sparrows, kestrels, house martins, buzzard, skylark and brown hare. Add to this 2 dead moles that I came across on 2 separate occasions. What happens to moles here?! Perhaps they pop up to witness the rich and varied wildlife and then succumb to it!

Wildflowers to be spotted through the year include, Red Campion, Greater Stitchwort, Bluebells, Buttercups, Yellow Archangel, Common Vetch, Herb Robert and further on in the field edges; Creeping Cinquefoil and the exquisite Scarlet Pimpernel.

On a warm sunny day you might also spot a few species of moth. I've seen Burnet moths, Silver Y, Nettle-tap and Silver-

ground Carpet, along with butterflies such as Meadow Brown, Large and Small Skippers, Ringlet, Peacock, Small Tortoiseshell, Comma, Red Admiral, Speckled Wood and many others all enjoying this wildlife haven. You might also be lucky enough to see a Dragonfly – most probably a Brown Hawker. If you keep your eyes peeled on a warm summer's day you'll certainly see Common Blue Damselflies.

Keep straight on for about 20-30 mins, ignoring any paths off L or R and eventually you'll arrive at a finger post at Hubbal Grange – a building which is no more, but nonetheless, an area of great historical importance.

An inscription on the post gives this information.

'Site of Hobbal Grange* behind you. Birthplace of the Penderel* Brothers. On 4-9-1651 King Charles II rested here after his defeat at the Battle of Worcester on the 3-9-1651. Presented by The Pendrill* Family History Society to commemorate the restoration of the monarchy May 29 1660-2010'.

As I write in 2013 I'm more than happy to report that the monarchy still exists!

(*There appears to be at least 3 ways of spelling Penderel, 2 of which appear in the few lines on the plaque! Also, and more curiously, the wording on the plaque has incorrectly named the house Hobbal Grange instead of Hubbal!)

④ Turn R here to walk with hedge and trees on R. Do NOT continue on the main path!

As you turn R, pause for a few seconds to imagine the scene as you glimpse, through the trees, the site of what would have been a quite splendid-looking house. In fact a fair bit of imagination is required here as the ruins of the timber-framed building are now overgrown by nettles and brambles.

(This section of the Monarch's Way branches off the main Monarch's Way because it was traversed in both directions by the fugitive prince as he backtracked in desperation to avoid capture).

Having turned R at the finger post, continue along the path passing a couple of separate oak trees on the R. Soon it turns into a wide farm track. Ignore all paths off until eventually the track swings R in front of a small copse.

STOP! ⑤   Don't follow the wide track! Be careful – it's easy to go wrong here!

Instead continue straight on at this corner to take the FP which goes slightly downhill, passing a pond on R, then a little zig-zag to walk with hedge on R.

Soon the track turns R towards Tong Park Farm and then L (it is waymarked) in the direction of the traffic noise that is the M54. At the end of the farm buildings the track runs onto a concrete lane, which then swings L and in a few yards sharp R, to pass under the motorway.

Out the other side leave the concrete drive behind to continue straight on with a pool on R. Follow the fence as it swings towards a pair of isolated houses with a magnificent lake in front and woodland on L.

This is the site of Shackerley Mill which was a flour mill until it burnt down in 1909. Nothing now remains and in fact one of the houses is built upon the site.

On reaching the houses the path turns L onto a drive which services the houses. Pass through a gate (signed on the other side Shackerley Mill) and soon pass RAF Cosford's barracks on R along this long straight lane.

⑥ On reaching a stop sign at a junction with a road turn R to walk along Sydnal Lane.

Towards the end of the lane you might want to pop in to the Spider's Web café for a quick drink and maybe a bite to eat.

At the end of the lane meet the busy A41 to cross via the pedestrian crossing at traffic lights and continue in the same direction by following the road opposite.

Pass by RAF Cosford's Outdoor Stadium on your left and eventually reach a railway bridge going over the road.

This is the Birmingham to Shrewsbury line and Cosford's train station for your return to Shifnal (Platform 2) but not before visiting RAF Cosford's excellent (and free!) Air Museum just along the road. Incidentally, there's also a small café here at the train station.

So... continue under the railway bridge as the road sweeps R

Soon you'll pass the Air Ambulance base which houses three distinctive helicopters resplendent in their red and yellow livery. They do such a fabulous job covering 6 counties and around 3000 missions every year (visit midlandsairambulance.com - a charity funded by people like us).

Shortly after, you'll arrive at the entrance to RAF Cosford's Air Museum.

There's quite a satisfying and somewhat smug feeling when you arrive here as, although the museum is totally free for all, the car park isn't – a fee we can ignore today!

Your first call might be tea, a sandwich and a well-earned rest at the café before exploring the museum itself – there's lots to see!   Website: raf.mod.uk/rafcosford

For your return simply retrace your steps to the train station (it's less than ½ a mile from the museum's entrance) and platform 2 for a train to Shifnal where on alighting, cross the line on the footbridge where the covered walkway down brings you right back into the centre of Shifnal to return you to your start point at the Millennium Clock.

Walk 23. Bridgnorth - linear.
River Worfe to River Severn

Distance: 15.2 miles
Time to allow: 7½ hrs without stops
Refreshments: Dog & Davenport pub at Worfe 4 miles from Bridgnorth plus a plethora of pubs and tea rooms in Bridgnorth itself.
Transport: Buses back to Shifnal from Bridgnorth Low Town or High Town.

This is a fabulous walk and one that should be considered by all walkers reading this book even if it's done in two sections over 2 separate days, but by far the best way is to do it in one go.

Jim, who tested this walk for me, declared it to be the best of the five he'd tested and he was surprised to find he came across not a soul all day until reaching Bridgnorth and meeting up with me at The Boatyard for a well-earned pint, on what was the hottest day of the year to date, in the summer of 2013.

From the lovely village of Ryton the route follows the River Worfe much of the way to its end, where it disgorges into the River Severn a little over a mile north of Bridgnorth.

There is a distinct sense of achievement and a feeling of great satisfaction upon reaching the River Severn at Bridgnorth especially if, by way of celebration, you then partake of a cuppa or a pint at one of the many hostelries.

NB: The map for this walk has been split into 3 stages for clarity and is marked in the text accordingly.

131

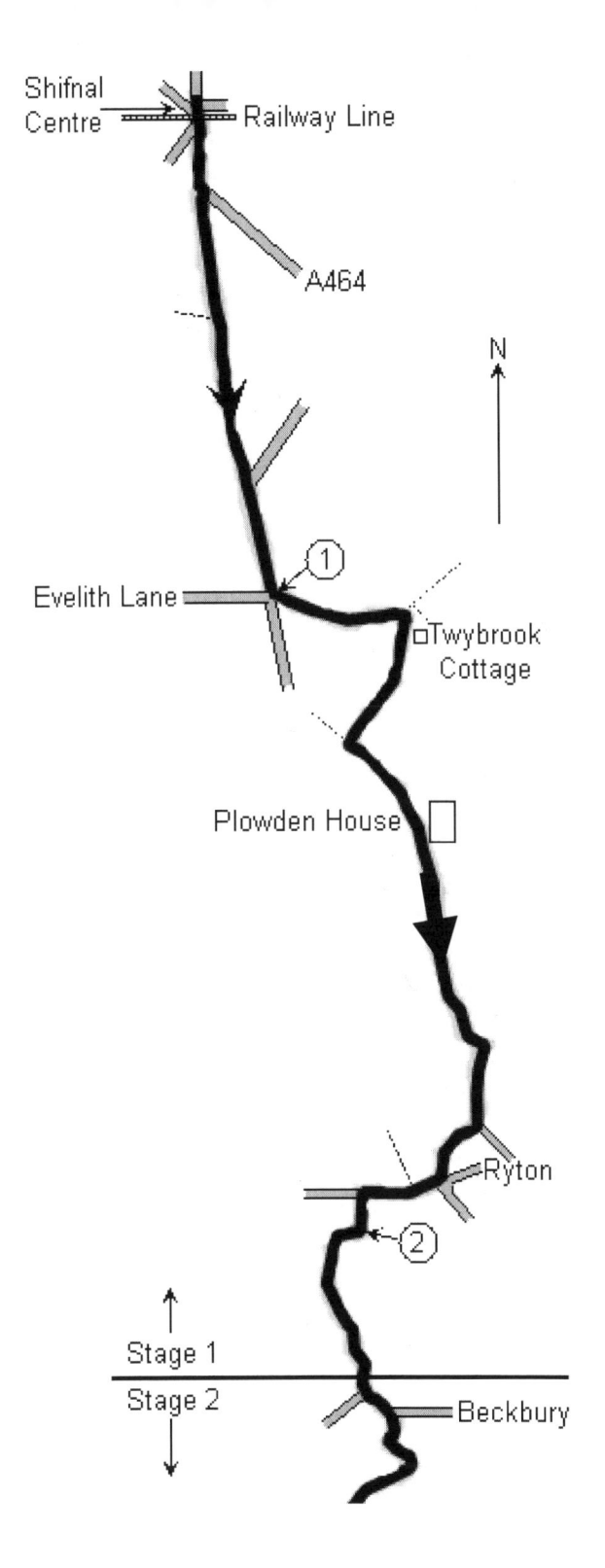

Stage 1 Map: Start the walk from the centre of Shifnal at the Millennium Clock and head south under the railway bridge, passing the Odfellows pub and the Park House Hotel on your left.

As the road bends L turn R up Park Lane (signed Ryton & Grindleforge), past St Andrews School and walk alongside a superb row of mature trees of oak, sycamore, holly, horse chestnut and beech. Soon the houses disappear as the lane narrows and becomes much quieter. Continue slightly down hill on this straight-as-a-die road until you reach Evelith Lane on the R <u>but don't turn up it</u>.

①
Turn L here down a long drive leading to a large house (although not visible at the start). At the gate take the FP to the R and follow it as it skirts the house and goes through a small wooded area, eventually reaching Twybrook Cottage.

Turn R here to pass in front of this lovely isolated cottage to follow a Permissive Path initially with hedge on L and once through a gate, follow with hedge on R. In a few short minutes arrive at another drive. Turn L here to pass by Plowden House *(built 1764 on the site of the original Hatton Grange)* behind which is woodland and host to a series of small but oddly named lagoons; Purgatory Pool, Abbot's Pool, Hell Pool and Bath Pool. Intriguing though they may be they're all out of bounds and out of sight to the public.

Follow the farm track for a further 20 minutes or so and cross what is known as Adamsford Bridge (although not marked as such).

This is our first encounter with the River Worfe, a stretch of water we will walk beside and cross many times as it meanders all the way to Bridgnorth.

Just after (and ignoring a makeshift style over barbed wire) take a sharp R at a hedge and follow the track which turns into a delightful sunken path. On emerging go through the gate and follow the FP to the lane at Ryton. Turn R here to walk past the church and descend to a crossroads where you turn R to walk along the lane, crossing the bridge over Wesley Brook.

Passing an old red phone box the lane climbs a short hill. As it levels out turn L to walk a wide, straight farm track with a metal gate at its end. Through the gate, stop and take stock:

②

Look half-right and through a large gap in the trees you should be able to see a stile in the hedge beyond, but because there's a valley between you and the stile you need to turn R and walk with hedge on R, cutting across the corner to reach said stile. This is at the head of a lovely valley that looks down towards Beckbury.

Stage 1 ↑
Stage 2 ↓

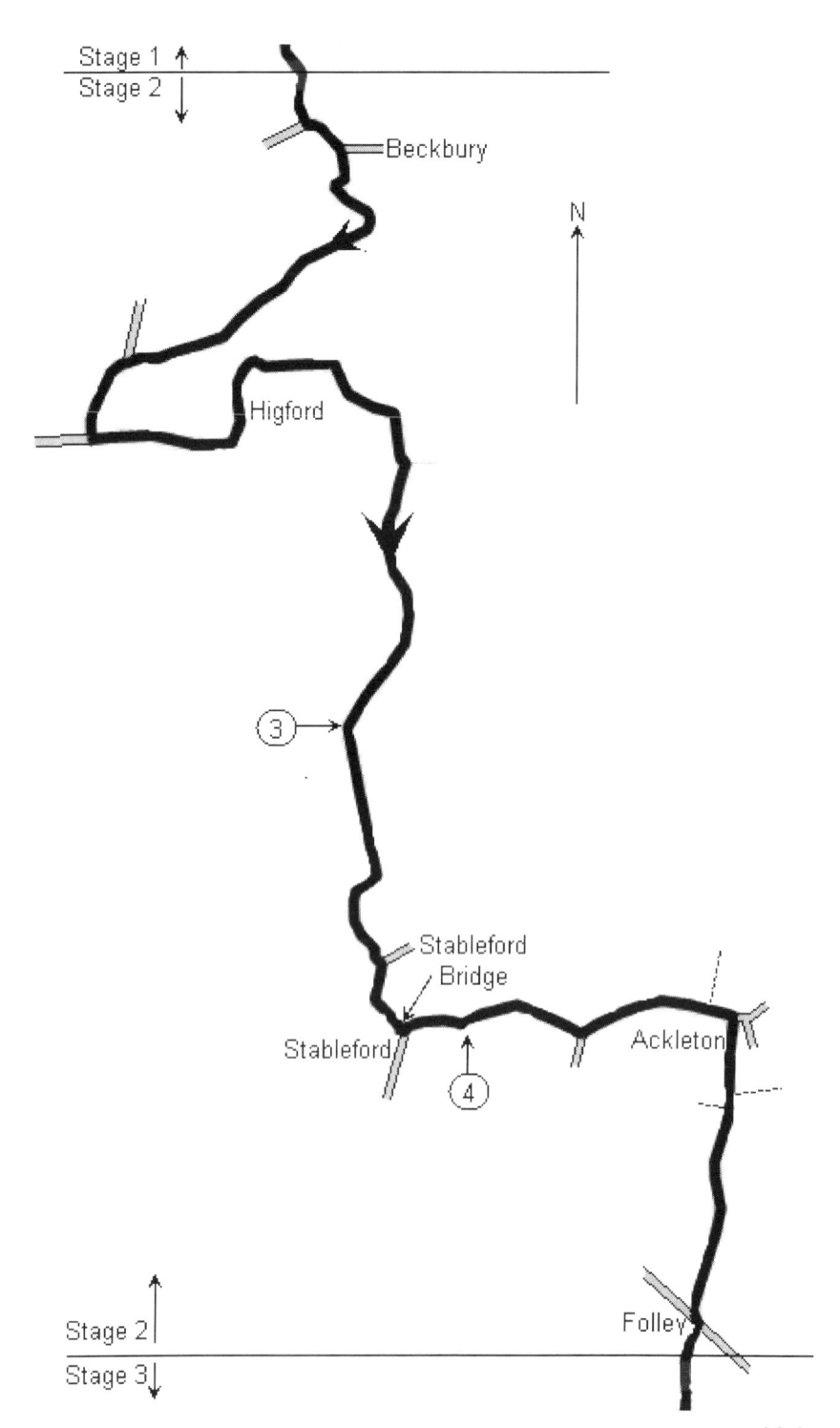

Beckbury

N ↑

Higford

③ →

Stableford Bridge
Stableford
Ackleton
④

Folley

Stage 2 ↑
Stage 3 ↓

Stage 2 Map:
Over the stile turn L to walk with hedge now on L. As the fence turns to the R climb the stile that comes into view and turn R with fence now on R. On reaching the trees turn L to head downhill keeping fence and now trees on R. Wesley Brook is still to be seen in the valley below. At the bottom of the trees turn R to follow the line of the fence and at a marker head towards a footbridge crossing a stream. This is Mad Brook.

Continue straight on to another footbridge, over what is quite often marshy ground. Turn slightly L and walk up through the field towards a house and stile to lane.

Turn L to walk down the lane and in a few yards take the BW on R and follow the obvious path (although in summer it may be less distinct due to vegetation) with pool on L, through a splendid bit of quintessential countryside.

This path is part of the 615 mile-long National Trail called the Monarch's Way. In the spring can be seen Greater Stitchwort, Buttercup and Bluebells, with Foxgloves forcing their way through along with Red Campion, White Dead Nettle and Cow Parsley in full bloom and in great abundance.

Eventually the BW goes through an equally enchanting bit of woodland and then deposits you onto a lane. Turn L to walk up the lane with hedgerow on L and field on R to reach a lane off L as the main lane bends R. *This is where we say goodbye to the Monarch's Way.* Our lane is signposted Cotsbroom (which is wrong – it should say Cotsbrook!) and Higford with a No Through Road sign. So turn L here up the lane, soon passing the remote Higford School.

This pleasant lane then descends cutting through sandstone rock, levels and then descends again swinging to the L with another No Through Road and a sat nav error notice too.

Soon the lane ends at a house on left and another on right. Our way goes straight ahead through the gate beyond.

Soon the sound of rushing water meets your ears as you cross the River Worfe again. Keep straight ahead, past a building on the right and onto a FP at the side of a rusty gate. Soon, at a path junction turn R to walk with the river on R through woodland. At another path junction turn R once again, soon climbing uphill.

At the top the path leaves woodland. Turn R to walk along a wide grassy track across a field. The path then swings L and then almost immediately turns R at a waymarked post and descends into a charming little valley, passing gorse bushes on the bank with, in the right season, the little blue-flowered Germander Speedwell near your feet.

Another waymarker confirms your route along this quite wide grassy track in the same general direction to the L of an old oak tree. Soon pass through a wide metal gate and into woodland once more with the River Worfe on the R.

Follow this wide sandy track and as it passes a large pool on right it rises <u>and when it swings L turn R</u> at a marker post through a large double metal gate into an open field with small hill on L and trees across the field to your R.

❸ The path goes ahead at the start and then swings gently L around the bottom of this small hill. Pass through another double metal gate and head towards a line of trees in front, keeping them to your R with a swampy area down to the R.

Soon arrive at another metal gate to enter woodland again (waymarker on post). Go straight on along a wide track eventually arriving at a lane.

Turn R to walk down the lane leading to Stableford. Just after crossing the River Worfe over the bridge take the FP off L near a telegraph pole to walk with hedgerow on R and the river on L.

You are now half-way to Bridgnorth.

Cross over the river again, this time on a footbridge. Pause here and take stock of the field ahead for this next instruction:

④ Carry on in the same direction (leaving the river behind) straight ahead up the hill through a gap between trees on R and gorse bushes on L, passing through another patch of gorse bushes on the way. (Ignore the gate into woodland on R. Just head straight to the top of the hill to a stile with waymarked post).

Climb the stile to walk with fence on R, eventually reaching a lane. Turn L to walk uphill soon arriving in Ackleton. Take the first lane on R (Folley Road), keeping on it as it rises and descends and ignoring all turns off until you reach a busy B road.

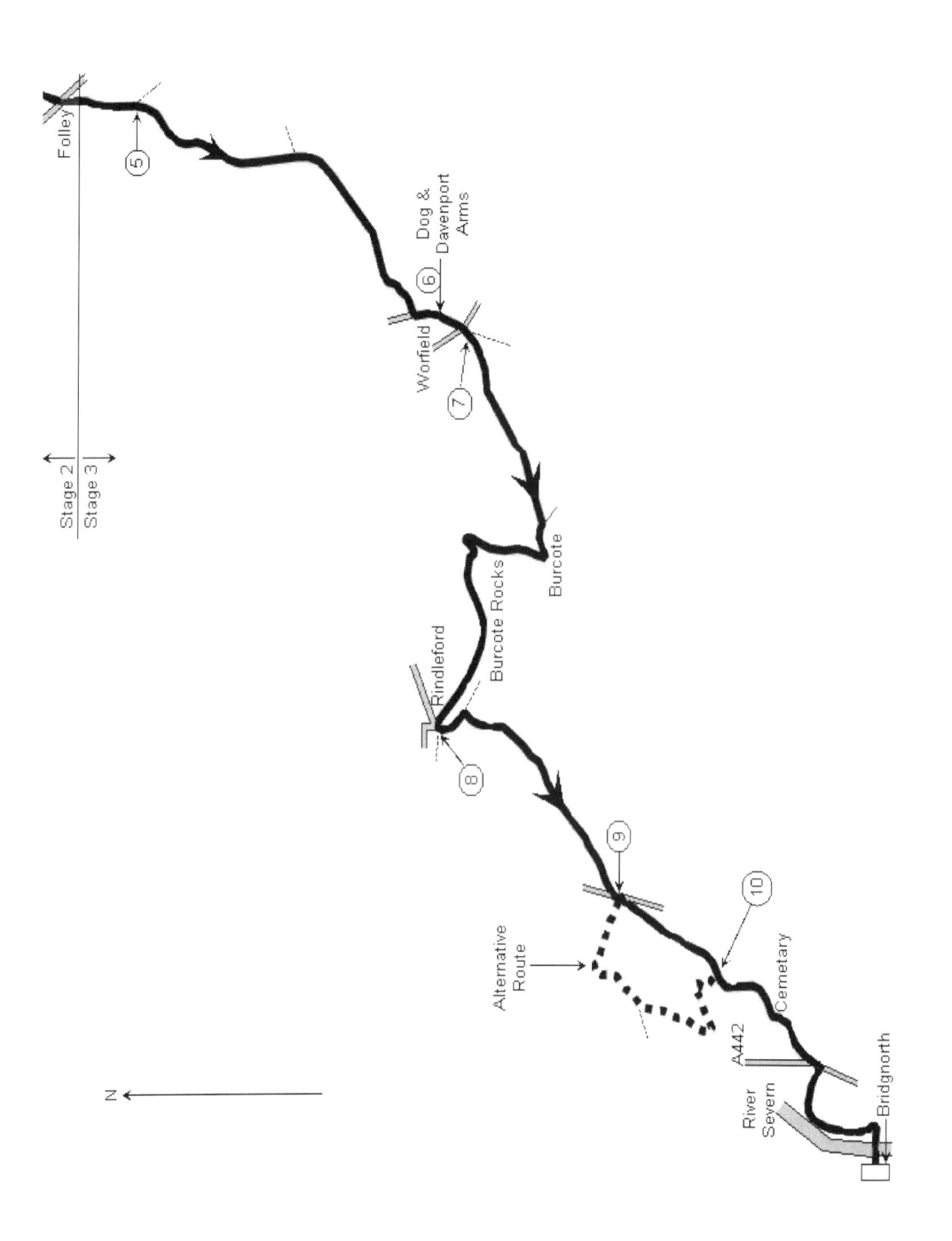

Stage 3 Map:
Turn L and in a few yards cross the road and take the FP on R through Folley Farm between house on L and farm buildings on R to a gate, to then walk with hedge on L with views across right to Brown Clee Hill – Shropshire's highest. The path then passes through hedgerows on both sides amass with Cow Parsley in the spring and a haven for butterflies on warm summer days.

⑤At a stile and gate you'll see a post with 2 waymarkers (may be overgrown in summer but passable). Follow the R arrow keeping the hedge you see in front of you on your R and descend to a gate at the bottom to walk with trees on L and pool on R.

At the end of the tree line go uphill on a wide track to another waymarker at a stile, to then walk with hedge on your L and then a fence.

At the next stile keep in the same direction straight across the field, heading to the L of a gate where you will soon see the stile in the fence. Cross a farm track to climb another stile to walk with small wooded area on R. Cross another stile to walk with fence on L and a view of Worfield's impressive church spire ahead.

When the fence ends carry straight on following the line of telegraph poles, to walk R of a fence to a stile on L and enter a garden nursery area, to walk with greenhouses and polytunnels on L with a line of trees on R.

Soon a lane is reached. Walk along this in the same direction where it soon swings R past a house and over the River Worfe again on a wide bridge. Pass a school on L and reach a road junction.

Turn L and walk along the road past The Dog & Davenport Arms.

⑥

If you've timed it right and checked opening times beforehand it might be time for refreshment – you're just 4 miles from Bridgnorth at this point. Or you may decide that you're so close now you may as well carry on and seek refreshment in Bridgnorth – the Boatyard pub by the River Severn is the most convenient as the route goes through its garden!.

Eventually reach another road junction past the tiny village green complete with war memorial. The signpost tells us to the R is Telford / Sutton Maddock and Claverley / Bridgnorth to the L. We're going neither way! Cross straight over to the FP opposite and climb the stile to walk with fence on R and then between the fence and a tree on your L.

⑦There are then 2 FP's. We need the R path which goes to the L of one tree and then to the R of the next tree slightly uphill.

Over the next stile the path crosses a narrow lane and goes a little more steeply uphill. At the top you'll see another marker at a fence corner. Follow the direction of it, crossing another narrow lane and head downhill to a gate and marker leading to the trees and the River Worfe below. Cross it on a footbridge, just L of a lone tree which you'll see near the corner of the field.

The remains of an old water mill can be seen here which was used to pump water up the hill you've just descended, to Davenport House, a Grade 1 listed Georgian mansion built in 1726.

Over the bridge turn R to walk with the river on your R and follow the path away from the river, to cross a stile into a field and a track, to soon pass a house. Walk between a house on R and building on L and through the gate to R of building with a stile beyond. Over the stile turn sharp R to walk behind the house on a narrow, but pleasant track, through a small copse and shortly the River Worfe below you to the R.

Out of the woodland keep on the path with the sandstone rock known as Burcote Rocks to your L. Follow closely the line of rocks as it swings L and then take the 'Alternative Path to avoid stile' at a house, up through woodland and down the other side to a lane which services the house. Walk along the lane, away from the house, over a bridge to shortly arrive on the edge of the delightful tiny hamlet of Rindleford.

⑧ Just before reaching the lane and houses, look for a FP on your L opposite a telegraph pole. As you walk along this path you will pass an impressive-looking mill on your right, now converted to a house. A footbridge takes you over the river and almost immediately another footbridge takes you over a tributary. This is a delightful path with the river to your L and Burcote Rocks to your R.

In just a few minutes take the BW going right-angles off R away from the river at a marker post and into the woodland (at the time of writing the post is loose and someone with a sense of perhaps misguided humour has turned the post so that the arrow points directly into the river!).

We must say goodbye now to the River Worfe which meanders westwards for a further 1.5 miles before merging with the River Severn.

This lovely path is a wonderful excursion into Shropshire's wildlife. On a warm summer's day you might be lucky to spot a damselfly called the Beautiful Demoiselle flitting along this exquisite woodland ride. Many butterflies enjoy this spot too with Comma, Peacock, Green-veined White and Small Tortoiseshell being amongst its visitors. Red Kite have also been spotted in the vicinity.

The path soon joins a wider track. Keep on in the same direction. Eventually you will pass a lovely old house on your R and another further on. Shortly you will reach a lane. Cross L to small grassy triangle and a FP sign.

⑨Here you have 2 options:
Either follow the obvious path up a wide farm track or take the less obvious FP ahead, up a short bank to a kissing gate at the side of a telegraph pole.

My suggestion is to spend about 5 minutes checking Option 1 first, by going up the short bank, through the kissing gate, cross a small scrubby field, then a farm track and through a gap in the hedge with a marker post.

What you're checking here is whether the path is passable or not, dependent on the field having either being ploughed, or in full crop. If it looks alright this is the shortest and easiest route (there may be an alternative by walking around the field perimeter).

Otherwise, return to the grassy triangle to take Option 2 following the more obvious FP along the wide track in the direction of the FP sign.

Please note; due to the somewhat precarious stretches on Option 2 this is most definitely unsuitable for children!

This path goes through woodland, is slightly longer (approx half-a-mile) and is certainly the more adventurous of the two as parts may be slightly overgrown with nettles and brambles (no real problem to those not wearing shorts!) whilst other parts have quite steep drops where a slip could result in a fall of several feet but easily negotiated with care.

However, in wet or icy conditions this would be much more difficult and best avoided. On the plus-side, there are fabulous views down to the River Severn and into Bridgnorth along the way.

I will describe both options, both meeting up eventually at a junction of paths.

Option 1. Having checked the field and found it passable (if it isn't, it's certainly worth reporting this to the local council) walk up through it keeping in the same direction, and heading just to the left of the tree line that you will see on the horizon, to a gate.

Keep in the same direction, passing a small squat building to your R. Walk down through the next field with woodland to your R which you will shortly enter. Then, after a few yards into the wood, at a path junction turn L.

⑩ When you reach a marker post with a swinging right hand path downhill <u>do not go down the path</u> but continue in the same direction.

Now go to ****** on page 145

Option 2. From the grassy triangle take the FP along a wide track with hedges on both sides, shortly passing 2 houses on your L. After the 2nd house leave the main track and continue in the same direction along a grassy one, towards woodland. This soon narrows and crosses a farm track to enter trees. (This is where it may be slightly overgrown but shouldn't present too much of a challenge). In a few yards the path opens up a little to reach woodland.

It was here that I once saw a weasel struggling to drag a dead pigeon along the path and presumably into its lair. I stood still as it headed towards me, completely oblivious to my presence, stopping every few inches to catch its breath, until it became aware that things weren't quite right and it quickly dashed into the undergrowth leaving its prey. I retreated and waited a few minutes to see it cautiously return and complete its mission.

From this point it takes around 45 minutes to reach the River Severn and Bridgnorth.

The path soon descends moving away from the woodland boundary on your left. When you reach a marker post don't take the path up L but continue to descend on the path R.

In a few yards arrive at another post at a fork, with several waymarks (including one for Worfield Walkers). Take the L fork uphill.

NB: Care is needed along this undulating and often quite narrow path as short stretches have steep drops to the right.

You'll soon hear the sound of traffic below to your right and the main road leading into Bridgnorth with tantalising glimpses of the River Severn below too. We're nearly there!

Eventually you'll reach an open area with a grassy slope leading down to a dangerous rocky precipice on your right with quite spectacular views into Bridgnorth.

> **CAUTION:** Don't be tempted to walk to the edge here - a drop of a hundred feet or more goes straight down to the main road!

So… cross straight over (ignoring the first path up L) to follow the main path as it swings gently round left and, in a few yards, crosses sandstone rocks still swinging gently left.

In the spring you'll pass through a large bank of heady aromatic Wild Garlic.

Eventually, after more undulations, the path rises and approaches the woodland boundary once more and a path junction at rocks. Turn R (more-or-less continuing in the same direction) and in a few minutes arrive at another path junction, this time with marker post. Turn R.

******

Options 1 & 2: (both routes meet here at the path junction)
After a short distance, a fork in the path is reached. Take the R path which goes steeply downhill through boulders either side. Glimpses of Bridgnorth can be caught through the trees and you'll also hear the traffic from the main road below.

You'll soon pass above a cemetery - first in front and then to your L - as you descend on a stepped path to the entrance of the cemetery at a small car park. Walk down the lane to the main road. Cross over to the L and turn R to walk through Severn Park down to the River Severn.

Our companion of this lovely walk for many miles - the River Worfe - is disgorging into the River Severn just over a mile north of here.

Turn L to walk alongside the river.

Look out for an interesting plaque at Hazledine's Foundry, signifying the site of the manufacture of the world's first fee-paying passenger locomotive in 1808.

Finally, as you approach the bridge, walk into the Boatyard pub garden where you may wish to end the walk with a very fine beverage or two along with a bite to eat. There are two other pubs just to the left as you approach the Boatyard pub; The Fosters Arms and The Vine.

To visit Bridgnorth Low Town continue up the steps to the bridge and turn R to cross the river.

If it's your intention to visit Bridgnorth High Town there are several ways to do so; the easiest, especially after a 15 mile walk is the charming Cliff Railway just on the other side of the bridge, which looks for all the world like a loaf of bread being hauled up the hillside!

If there's time and you have the energy there's lots to do in this fine old market town but my guess is you're in need of a good rest after your exertions so take a seat and enjoy your well-earned refreshments!

Oh…and well done!